6.—

DATE DUE

MAR 0 4 2002		
11-19-08		

GAYLORD PRINTED IN U.S.A.

The Brazilian Revolution of 1930 and the Aftermath

Bogotá
COLOMBIA
VENEZUELA
GUIANAS
Cayenne
ATLANTIC OCEAN
Equator
Boa Vista
RORAIMA TERRITORY
AMAPÁ TERRITORY
Macapá
Negro R.
IS. of MARAJÓ
Belém
Manaus
Amazon R.
Solimões R.
Tapajós R.
Xingu R.
Tocantins R.
São Luís
Iquitos
Madeira R.
Fortaleza
Teresina
CEARÁ
RIO GRANDE DO NORTE
Natal
MARANHÃO
Araguaia R.
PARÁ
PARAÍBA
João Pessôa
AMAZONAS
PIAUÍ
PERNAMBUCO
Recife
PERU
Porto Velho
ALAGOAS
Maceió
ACRE
Rio Branco
São Francisco R.
SERGIPE
Aracaju
RONDÔNIA TERRITORY
BOLIVIA
BAHIA
Salvador
MATO GROSSO
GOIÁS
Ilhéus
Federal District
BRASÍLIA
Cuiabá
Goiânia
Montes Claros
Corumbá
MINAS GERAIS
Belo Horizonte
ESPÍRITO SANTO
Tietê R.
Ouro Prêto
Vitória
PARAGUAY
SÃO PAULO
Volta Redonda
RIO DE JANEIRO
Paraná R.
Ourinhos
Campinas
Niterói
São Paulo
Rio de Janeiro
Santos
GUANABARA
Itararé
PARANÁ
Asunción
Curitiba
SANTA CATARINA
Uruguay R.
Santo Ângelo
Florianópolis
São Luís
Passo Fundo
São Borja
Itaqui
RIO GRANDE DO SUL
Uruguaiana
Pôrto Alegre
Alegrete
Santa Maria
ARGENTINA
Pelotas
Lagoa dos Patos
URUGUAY
Buenos Aires
Montevideo
Rio de la Plata
N
0
500
1000
MILES

Brazil

JORDAN M. YOUNG

The Brazilian Revolution of 1930 and the Aftermath

Barry College Library
Miami, Florida

Rutgers University Press
New Brunswick, New Jersey

Copyright © 1967 by Rutgers, The State University

Library of Congress Catalogue No.: 66-25171

Manufactured in the United States of America by
the Quinn & Boden Company, Inc., Rahway, N.J.

68248

F
2538
.Y6

To Dionir

Preface

October 24, 1930, is a dividing point in Brazilian history. The first republican government of Brazil, in existence for forty-one years, suddenly collapsed. The nation fell under the domination of politicians from Rio Grande do Sul, Brazil's southernmost state.

Getúlio Vargas, leader of the new group, profoundly changed the national political style. There was one Brazil before 1930, another emerged during the fifteen years that Vargas and his political lieutenants controlled the country. The transformation was not an easy one. Complex problems resulting from the dislocation of traditional social and economic forces by the revolution continue into the contemporary period. Every major shift in the political affairs of Brazil from 1930 to 1966 has represented either a defense of Getúlio Vargas or an attack on the man and the forces he brought into politics.

This book provides some of the hard political facts that went into the planning, maneuvering and execution of the successful 1930 revolt. There is still much research to be done before the historical record can be set straight. Meantime, I hope that this volume will help to separate some of the myths from the realities of contemporary Brazilian history.

The political form that is emerging today in Brazil must, because of the 1930 revolution, accommodate larger segments of the population. Before 1930, a small elite controlled the nation. Major political decisions were made by conservative leaders representing the interests of the states of São Paulo and Minas Gerais almost exclusively. Domestic tranquility was achieved by an effective alliance of the military and the Paulista and Mineiro politicians. It was shared power; part civilian, part military. The situation changed dramatically in 1930 when the São Paulo elite and the Minas Gerais leaders were shunted aside by the Gaúchos from Rio Grande do Sul. To neutralize these two states Vargas had to construct a new political power base.

When Vargas was toppled in 1945, many thought that Brazil would return to pre-1930 political arrangements, with the Paulista and Mineiro politicians again assuming control. This was not to be the case. The fifteen Vargas years had destroyed the traditional political structure of the nation. Along with a general awakening experienced by the urban population, the military had been given a taste of power by the success of the 1930 revolt and from 1945 on they were to play an ever increasing role in the affairs of the nation.

From 1945 to 1966 there has been a search for stability and a search also for a political structure that would answer the legitimate demands of millions of Brazilians in all parts of the country. That this political system has not yet been found is obvious. But the key to understanding the uneasiness in Brazilian political life today is to be found in the changes brought about by the 1930 revolution. The allegiance of the "new" Brazilians to the political process must be won before stability can be achieved.

My interest in Brazilian affairs began in 1941 when I took a "Junior Year" at the University of São Paulo and the Escola Livre de Sociologia e Política de São Paulo. Shortly after World War II began I worked as a rural sociologist in the Special Public Health Service (SESP), which was organized by Nelson Rockefeller's Office of Inter-American Affairs. For nearly eighteen months my assignments took me into the interior of Brazil. In 1949 I returned to Brazil with a United States Office of Education fellowship to do research on the 1930 revolution.

Much of the raw material about the revolution is to be found in Pôrto Alegre, capital of the state of Rio Grande do Sul. The city was the headquarters for most of the planning and operations. The citizens of Pôrto Alegre take great pride in the revolution and still feel, more than thirty years after the event, that October, 1930, was "their revolution." The archives, newspapers and magazines and the personal correspondence of nearly every citizen carry poignant memories of this finest hour in Rio Grande do Sul history. While in Pôrto Alegre I microfilmed most of the important newspapers published in

1929 and 1930. Though many people gave me excellent suggestions, it was Walter Spaulding, a Rio Grande do Sul historian, who was especially helpful in leading me to valuable collections of documents.

While I was working in Pôrto Alegre in October 1949, Vargas heard of my research project and invited me to his ranch at São Borja for a *churrasco* and conversation. I was pleased, especially since I knew that Getúlio Vargas had no special warmth for North Americans, but, as my luck would have it, I could not accept the invitation. Vargas had just announced his candidacy for the March, 1950, presidential elections and my advisers in the State Department suggested that my visit might possibly be misconstrued in diplomatic quarters.

The archives of the São Paulo municipal library contain detailed accounts of the damages caused by the invading troops from Rio Grande do Sul, but Paulistas would rather not discuss 1930. They feel that they were unjustly treated by the new revolutionary government. It is interesting to note that since 1930 no São Paulo political leader has occupied the presidency of Brazil, with the exception of Jânio Quadros, the incumbent for seven months in 1961. For the Paulistas, the 1932 rebellion against the Vargas Administration is the high point of their twentieth century history.

Moving on to Rio de Janeiro in December, 1949, I found many of the Gaúcho political leaders who had arrived with Vargas in 1930, and could not bring themselves to return to Pôrto Alegre. This gave me the opportunity to discuss with them various aspects of the 1930 revolution.

Osvaldo Aranha, a close personal friend of Vargas' and his Minister of Finance, read what I had written by that time about the events of 1930 and felt that it presented an accurate description of the scene. To flesh out some of the details he opened his then unorganized archives to me. (Since then, I understand, his files have been carefully catalogued.) In my many visits with him I met other participants in the events of 1930, for Aranha's house was always overflowing with political friends who delighted in reenacting various scenes of the revolution. Aranha's warm personality and exuberance were obviously undimmed after more than a quarter of a century of political life. It was easy to picture him as the dynamo of the revolution in Rio Grande do Sul. Never cautious, he must have tried the patience of men like Getúlio Vargas and General

Pedro Aurélio Góes Monteiro, who kept their political passions under tight control.

João Neves da Fontoura also read my preliminary manuscript and carefully called my attention to the role of the Congress (located then in Rio de Janeiro). Neves felt that the success of the revolution had hinged a great deal on the enthusiasm and interest generated by the speeches of Liberal Alliance politicians in the Congress—all carefully reported by the Rio de Janeiro press in 1929 and 1930. The climate of opinion in the city of Rio de Janeiro must always be given special attention in evaluating the political events of the nation.

A prominent Minas Gerais political leader, Odilon Braga, who also read my manuscript in 1949, made some pertinent suggestions concerning the role of the Mineiros in the revolution.

General Góes Monteiro, whom I interviewed later in Washington, D.C., analyzed various aspects of the impact of the military on the political affairs of the nation. He felt that the armed forces had to play a special role, a role they could not avoid. The army was the national conscience and moderating power. In discussing the battle of Itararé, the general refused to budge from the position that it was a nasty and decisive event in the revolution of 1930. This viewpoint is, of course, disputed by most Brazilians. Góes Monteiro, in the author's opinion, was one of the most underestimated men in Brazilian affairs from 1930 to 1945.

The 1930 revolution remains controversial in contemporary Brazil. Many of the important figures in the 1964 revolution were the young lieutenants of 1930. They are now playing out a final phase of their political careers in the service of the new government. Such familiar names as Juarez Távora, Eduardo Gomes and Juraci Magalhães constantly appear in the inner circles of the revolutionary regime. Perhaps the young army men who felt cheated by the 1930 revolution are finally having their turn in governing Brazil. I asked Juraci Magalhães in 1962 whether he believed the 1930 revolution had been good for Brazil. He answered emphatically that it had been necessary and that he would do it all over again. In 1964, he and others collaborated closely with the anti-Goulart forces to overturn the government.

I should like to thank Professor Engel Sluiter of the University of California, Berkeley, for always demanding more facts and extra proof of the events described.

A word about the spelling of Brazilian names in this book. The "new orthography" of Brazil lays down certain rules, but Brazilians characteristically refuse to be regimented. Some Brazilians and some Brazilian publishers follow the rules, others do not. Thus, the names of prominent people may be spelled in several different ways in both books and documents. In the body of this book I have tried to follow the modern orthography. I have also followed a time-honored Brazilian custom whereby certain men prominent in public life are commonly known by their Christian names rather than by their family names. References in the text are indexed under both.

The Brazilian revolution of 1930 and the subsequent thirty-six years of national history are full of unanswered questions. Although I have listened carefully and weighed the suggestions of many Brazilian friends, the responsibility for my interpretations of events must fall squarely on my own shoulders.

JORDAN M. YOUNG

Princeton, New Jersey
October, 1966

Contents

The Brazilian Revolution of 1930 and the Aftermath

Chapter 1

The Colonial and Imperial Background

> The people are starving and oppressed. Representative government has been destroyed by the oligarchies and the professional politicians. Brutality, violence and squandering of public funds is seen at every level of Brazilian national politics. . . . We have begun a counter-revolution to regain liberty, to restore the purity of the republican regime, to reconstruct the nation. The state of Rio Grande do Sul stands up for all of Brazil. We cannot evade our heroic destiny.[1]

This proclamation on October 4, 1930, by Getúlio Vargas, governor of the state of Rio Grande do Sul, signaled the beginning of a rebellion against the federal government and brought a period of Brazilian history to an abrupt close. Twenty-three days later the horses of Rio Grande do Sul Gaúcho troops were securely tied to the obelisk in downtown Rio de Janeiro, the capital of the nation, and a new era of Brazilian history and politics opened. Though the tying of the horses to the obelisk may have been symbolic, it also meant concretely that the soldiers, the politicians and the citizens of the state of Rio Grande do Sul were taking a commanding position in the Brazilian political and economic structure. In doing this they were, however briefly, also speaking and acting for much of Brazil.

When the proclamation was issued from Pôrto Alegre, capital of Rio Grande do Sul, against the government of President Washington Luís, and echoed in the states of Minas Gerais and Paraíba, it struck a sympathetic chord in every section of the country and was well received on nearly every level of Brazilian political, economic and social life. Brazilians wanted a political change. The fifteen-year Vargas period, ushered in by the arrival of the Gaúcho troops in Rio de Janeiro, dramatically informed the nation that this change had occurred. These changes provide the framework for the government of present-day Brazil.

The course of Brazilian history has been and continues to be consistently different from that of the other countries of the Hispanic world. By the sixteenth century, Portugal, unlike Spain, had developed a pattern of cosmopolitanism and a spirit of racial and religious toleration, and the political evolution of Brazil was less violent than that of the Spanish American colonies. Bloodshed and terrorism are alien to the Brazilian historical process.

When Pedro Álvares Cabral planted the royal standard of Dom Manoel I of Portugal on Brazilian soil in April, 1500, the Portuguese were not unprepared for the problems they would face in governing this new land. For nearly a hundred years before the Brazilian discovery they had successfully experimented in Africa with various types of economic and political operations, and these were later applied in Brazil.[2] Trading posts were set up along the coast and brazilwood, valued in Europe as a dye, was shipped to Portugal. Very quickly the Portuguese administrators understood that the country was poor and yielded little in gold, diamonds or spices. In view of the limited manpower and meager financial resources of Portugal, the decision was made to neglect Brazil and to concentrate on Africa and the Far East, both wealthy in slaves and spices. This made Brazil seem an easy acquisition for other European powers seeking footholds in the New World.

In an effort to make the country more attractive to Portuguese investors and prevent it from falling into non-Portuguese hands, the Crown in 1534 divided Brazil into fifteen captaincies, somewhat similar to seventeenth-century English proprietary colonies. The owner of a captaincy, a *donatário*, was given almost complete economic and political control over his colony. But agriculture was not profitable, and despite these inducements only two captaincies, Pernambuco and São Vicente, prospered. In 1549 the Portuguese government created the captaincy-general of Brazil in an attempt to reorganize the lagging colony and turn it into a profitable and attractive venture.[3] This move also failed.

The activities of the Portuguese clergy are in sharp contrast to the stumbling and ineffective measures of the political authorities. The Jesuit Manoel da Nobrega, who went to Brazil in 1549, was the first of many exceptional religious leaders who played important and often decisive roles in the history of the country.[4] Though the Jesuits failed in their attempt to protect the Indians from the colonists, they did manage to extend their influence by becoming advisers to the political authorities, setting up convents, seminaries, colleges and, later, universities. Education of the elite was exclusively in the hands of the Church.

The Portuguese Catholicism that was carried to Brazil was more moderate and more humane than Spanish Catholicism.[5] It soon developed a peculiar blend of softness, pliability and permissiveness that enabled an intimate and mutually satisfactory Church-State relationship to develop. Ecclesiastical authorities were often the only binding elements in the early formative period of Brazilian history. The events of 1580 to 1640 did little to change this situation.

When King Sebastian of Portugal died in 1578 leaving no heirs, Cardinal Henrique occupied the throne until Philip II of Spain, through bribery, battle and legitimate claim, added Portugal and her overseas possessions to his vast empire in 1580. Spanish domination of Portugal from 1580 to 1640 had two distinct and far-reaching effects on Brazilian historical development.

First the Dutch, bitter enemies of Spain, invaded Brazil. They failed in their first attempt to establish a foothold in Bahia in 1624, but were successful in 1630, when they captured the Pernambuco colony, and ultimately controlled over twelve hundred miles of Brazilian coastline before their expulsion in 1654.[6] Even though Portugal won her freedom from Spain in 1640, the Portuguese did not come to the aid of the Brazilian colonists battling the Dutch invaders. Thus, the defeat of the Dutch is hailed as a national victory in which the first glimmer of an emerging nationalism can be discerned.

The second effect of Spanish domination was the appearance of an amazing group of self-contained, exploring and slave-hunting bands called Bandeirantes. Operating from the southeastern São Paulo region, they pushed Brazilian frontiers further inland every decade, and later in the 1690's struck a valuable gold area in the state of Minas Gerais.[7] The Portuguese were also expanding into the Amazon area, with the founding of the town of Belém do Pará in 1616.

The expansion in the north and the discovery of gold extended the frontiers of Brazil and repeated earlier patterns of economic activity. Up to 1700 economic activity had been concentrated in the sugar plantations hugging the fertile coastal areas. The demand for Indian slaves had opened the interior. Now the attention of the Brazilian would turn further inland and to the south. Gold became a powerful magnet pulling colonists from all the other sections of the country. The population of the state of Minas Gerais swelled, and the cities of Rio de Janeiro and São Paulo throbbed with commercial activity. The political and economic activity of Brazil shifted from the sugar plantations in the north to the southeast, and in 1763 the capital of Brazil was moved from Bahia to Rio de Janeiro.

In the last years of the eighteenth century, however, Brazil was still a slow-moving, economically and politically backward area. The state of Minas Gerais provided the first serious indication that all was not well in relations between Portugal and Brazil. As in the British colonies, taxation was the surface reason for protest. The real problems were much deeper. The Portuguese demanded exorbitant taxes from the gold-producing areas and harshly suppressed any complaints as politically inspired. Inept and corrupt governors sent from Portugal created a spirit of revolt among the young elite of the wealthy families of Minas Gerais. One of the leading conspirators, Joaquim José da Silva Xavier (Tiradentes), was determined to fight Portuguese tyranny. He and other young revolutionaries made plans to separate Brazil from Portugal. But the conspiracy was betrayed in 1789 and the Portuguese Crown crushed the movement ruthlessly. After a two-year trial, Tiradentes was sentenced to death and the other conspirators were given lighter sentences. The Brazilian reaction was not at all what the Crown had anticipated. Tiradentes became a martyr and his death had much more significance than his original conspiracy. As a result, tax-collection methods were changed and the crisis between colony and mother country seemed to be over.

In 1800 Brazil was still living in splendid isolation. Generally ignored by Portugal and the rest of the world, 3,250,000 Brazilians inhabited nearly half the continent of South America. Figures for this period are unreliable, but the population probably included over 1,500,000 Negro slaves, nearly 500,000 Indians and approximately 600,000 of mixed racial background.[8] This was a tight slave-plantation society, a tiny white elite at the top of a social pyramid, and a huge illiterate population, relatively peaceful and submissive.

Napoleon Bonaparte's orders for the invasion of Portugal in 1807 were to disrupt the peace and quiet of Brazil. The Prince Regent of Portugal, later Dom João VI, decided to flee the invading French army and to take refuge in the New World colony of Brazil. The British, in control of the high seas, were only too eager to help. On November 29, 1807, English ships of war were in the harbor of Lisbon ready to escort a Portuguese fleet of sixteen vessels that would carry the refugee royal court to Brazil.

Dom João and his very unpopular wife, the Princess Carlota Joaquina, daughter of Charles IV of Spain, hastily embarked with fifteen hundred members of the court. After nearly two months at sea, the royal party arrived in Bahia on January 23, 1808, and then continued down to Rio de Janeiro. In both cities Brazilians warmly welcomed the Portuguese.

This is the most important event in the development of a Brazilian historical pattern. It weighs more than any other in the balance of any attempt to explain the difference between Brazilian history and that of other Latin American countries.

The arrival of the royal court resulted in the maintenance of a political system that was slowly fading in Europe. Though this transplant was very Portuguese, it was subtly changed and molded by Brazilian realities. In the other Latin American countries the years of the viceroys were numbered. While Brazil peacefully adjusted to European royalty, most of the countries under Spanish domination were torn apart internally and by the attempt of Spain to prevent their independence. The European-Portuguese political structure persisted until 1889, when finally New World history caught up with Brazil. The breathing spell was significant and extremely valuable.

The years that Dom João VI spent in Brazil, from 1808 to 1821, profoundly affected the country. Reforms were decreed and the commercial monopoly that had prevented Brazil from trading with other countries was eliminated. On January 28, 1808, the ports of Brazil were opened to the friendly nations of the world. Industries that had been restricted were now permitted to flourish. The impulse for a tiny entrepreneurial class was developing.[9] The first printing presses were sanctioned; the Bank of Brazil, two medical schools and a military and naval college were founded. In December, 1816, Brazil was raised to the status of a kingdom when the "United Kingdom of Portugal, Brazil and Algarves" was proclaimed.

In sharp contrast with these actions were the scandalous extravagance of the Portuguese court and the intrigues of Carlota Joaquina. The Princess' ill-concealed contempt for Brazil and constant plotting with Spanish authorities in the Uruguay and Rio Grande do Sul areas resulted in a steadily rising sentiment of distrust and dissatisfaction with Portuguese royalty. But the positive aspects of the period are far more significant. The various reforms of Dom João shook Brazil from her colonial frame of mind. Citizens felt a sense of pride in being Brazilian and in sheltering their King. Brazil during the period that Dom João VI spent in that country had taken great psychological strides toward independence.

With the defeat of Napoleon in 1814, a curious situation developed as Dom João VI showed no desire to return to Portugal. The British military, awaiting his return, set up and supported a Regency in Portugual. In 1817 Portuguese patriots rose in revolt against this unpopular Regency, with the result that British Marshal William Carr Beresford executed twelve of the ringleaders. Another revolution in 1820 forced the Regency out and brought the proclamation of a constitution similar to the liberal Spanish document of 1812. The victors issued a demand that the King return from Brazil or forfeit his kingdom. On April 26, 1821, Dom João VI appointed his son Dom Pedro Prince Regent of Brazil and reluctantly returned to Portugal. It has often been reported that he gave his twenty-three-year-old son the following advice: "If the worse come to the worst and Brazil demands independence, proclaim it yourself and put the crown on your own head."

Shortly after the King returned to Lisbon, Portuguese politicians re-enacted the scene that the British Parliament had played with the North American colonies in the 1770's. The Portuguese Côrtes failed to recognize that positive and independent attitudes toward the mother country had developed in Brazil between 1808 and 1821, and on September 29, 1821, it issued two orders that triggered the Brazilian independence movement. The first closed local Brazilian courts and transferred their operations to Portugal. The other ordered the very popular Prince Regent, Pedro, to transfer his control of the government to a junta of Portuguese officials, and return to Europe to finish his education. These orders arrived in Brazil on December 10, 1821, and caused an uproar. Brazilians rallied to the Prince Regent, requesting that he remain in Brazil and declare the country independent. One of the most articulate advocates of the policy was the Paulista José Bonifácio de Andrada e Silva. On January 9, 1822, a petition was signed by over eight thousand citizens requesting Pedro not to return to Portugal. Pedro declared he would remain in Brazil.

Political leaders in São Paulo and Minas Gerais began to mobilize public opinion in favor of an open declaration of independence. When Pedro received dispatches from Lisbon indicating that the Portuguese Côrtes would not consider any changes in policy regarding Brazil, Pedro made his decision. On September 7, 1822, Pedro declared Brazil an empire, independent of Portugal.

Though Portugal tried feebly to prevent Brazil's independence, she followed the lead of the United States and Great Britain and recognized the new state in 1825.

Independence had taken place with relatively little bloodshed and violence. There were no waves of destruction and the social order remained stable. No one sector of the population suffered wounds that would fester in the body politic and poison the developing nation at a later period. A dramatic change had taken place in Brazilian political history and no one suffered. This event placed one more stone in the concept of the Brazilian regarding the peaceful historical and the political process in his country. These are the binding elements that affect Brazil today.

The nine years between 1822 and 1831, when Dom Pedro I reigned as Emperor of Brazil, were not easy ones. An impetuous and unruly monarch, Pedro did not agree with the attempts of civilian political leaders to limit his powers through a constitution. He dissolved a constituent assembly that had been elected to write a Brazilian constitution and ordered a council of state under his control to prepare the fundamental charter for the nation. Thus, the Constitution of 1824 was a creation of Dom Pedro I, given to the Brazilian people by the monarch, rather than a constitution written by a sovereign people for themselves. This action was no great step forward in self-government.

The major lines of the Constitution reveal an effective and workable document that was used to govern Brazil until 1889. Brazil was declared an hereditary constitutional monarchy under the House of Bragança. Three branches of government were created: legislative, executive and judicial. The Parliament was composed of two houses, members being elected indirectly. Senators had life membership, members of Chamber of Deputies served for four years. The country was divided into provinces governed by presidents appointed by and responsible to the Emperor. Each province, however, had an assembly for consultative purposes whose members were elected and served for four years. Freedom of speech and press were guaranteed. Roman Catholicism was declared the official religion of the State.

The most interesting and significant aspect of the charter was the *poder moderador*, the moderating power of the Emperor. Chapter 5 of the Constitution, which granted this power, is the key to the whole structure of Brazilian political life from 1824 to 1889. It enumerated one hundred powers of the Emperor. Among them were the naming of senators taken from a list of three who had been elected by the provincial assemblies, calling the Senate and the Chamber into session, dissolving the Senate and the Chamber, authorizing laws between sessions and nominating and removing ministers of state.[10] Throughout the period that the 1824 Constitution was in effect, the chief of state, whether Dom Pedro I or II, could not be countermanded.

Despite this power, Pedro I did not govern well. Imbued with the traditions of the Old World aristocracy and in constant conflict with the New World political process, Pedro lost his popularity quickly and constantly irritated the Brazilians. In 1824 a revolt developed in the northeastern province of Pernambuco. Though crushed in six months, it resulted in the weakening of the allegiance of the Brazilians in this area to the Emperor. The creation of an independent Uruguay in 1824 ended Brazil's dream of dominating the La Plata Basin, and the prestige of the Emperor fell as a result of this loss.

Relations between the Brazilian legislature and the monarch worsened in 1826 when King João VI died and Dom Pedro I fell heir to the crown of Portugal. Pedro abdicated his right, but declared that his daughter Maria da Glória was heir to the Portuguese throne. When civil war broke out in Portugal, Pedro I became deeply and constantly involved in Portuguese politics, to the annoyance and distaste of his Brazilian subjects.

Tension mounted as the press violently criticized the Emperor, disorders broke out in the capital of the country, and finally the army took sides with the civilians in opposing the actions of the monarch. On April 7, 1831, Pedro I abdicated the throne of Brazil in favor of his five-year-old son, Pedro de Alcântara, and returned to Portugal, where he died in 1834. The Brazilian Parliament appointed a Regency to govern the country until Pedro reached his majority.

The years 1831 to 1840 were the most crucial and dangerous in Brazilian history. The country was in a state of almost complete anarchy. A few political leaders struggled to keep the nation together. The most important, José Bonifácio de Andrada e Silva, had been ordered by the departing King to serve as tutor and guardian of young Pedro. The 1824 Constitution had provisions for a Regency to govern the country until Pedro reached eighteen. Of the four Regencies between 1831 and 1840, those of Padre Diogo Antônio Feijó, 1835 to 1837, and Pedro Araújo Lima, 1837 to 1840, were the most significant.

The expected fragmentation of Brazil in this crisis period never took place. Yet the signs of a crumbling national state were everywhere. Revolts against the Rio de Janeiro government took place in the states of Pará and Minas Gerais in 1831 and 1833 respectively. The states of Mato Grosso and Maranhão followed this pattern in 1834. In 1835 a Mohammedan Negro revolt took place, and there began a frankly separatist movement in Rio Grande do Sul that was to last for ten years.

What kept the nation a single unit during this period is a baffling question; however, the vast size of the country often permitted local solutions to problems even though they ran counter to laws decreed in the national capital. Brazil was re-enacting the historical process that had permitted the country as a colony of Portugal to seek in many ways her own destiny and arrive at her own solutions to Portuguese administrative and economic demands when such demands made no sense in Brazil. Now the process was repeating itself with the capital or the heart of Brazil, Rio de Janeiro and São Paulo, in conflict with the other areas. The outlying regions of Pará, Pernambuco, Bahia and Rio Grande do Sul were faced with different problems and had different responses to their political and economic questions. In 1834 the Regency adjusted to political realities. Parliament passed a law giving more power to provincial legislatures, which added to the developing sense of federalism in some of the more important provinces. In Parliament a small elite group, though divided into Conservatives and Liberals, had a main aim of keeping Brazil from fragmenting into many independent countries, as had occurred in other South American areas. Pragmatic, they felt that political survival came before republican experiments.

Toward the end of the Regency period Liberal party political leaders, disturbed by the increasing intransigence of their Conservative party opponents, passed a bill in Parliament in April, 1840, which permitted Pedro to take the throne although he was only fifteen. The Liberals felt that they would benefit and that the nation would be held together by the accession of young Dom Pedro II. He was crowned on July 18, 1841.[11]

Dom Pedro II ruled Brazil from 1841 to 1889. Both Liberals and Conservatives supported the young Emperor, as did the highest-ranking army officer, General Luís Alves de Lima e Silva, later named the Duque de Caxias. The first decade was taken up with the suppression of civil wars and the consolidation of the Emperor's power. The political stability during the forty-eight years of Dom Pedro II's reign hinged on two points. The first was the character and personality of the Emperor. Dom Pedro was exceptionally well trained and talented. He apparently understood his role and took his assignment as Emperor of Brazil very seriously. The second point was his skillful use and application of the *poder moderador*. Though it gave him absolute power, he used it sparingly. In the 1870's the Emperor permitted the Parliament to curb some of his powers, but until the very last years of his reign Dom Pedro governed Brazil.

The two political parties, the Liberals and the Conservatives, carefully respected the rules of the political structure. Both parties represented a small elite. There was no economic conflict between the two, in that the wealth of most Liberals and Conservatives generally came from large landholdings. Throughout most of the Dom Pedro II period there was no challenge to the power structure in a political or economic sense from newer, broader-based groups with wealth and power earned in commercial areas.

Illiteracy was extremely high, and property qualifications for voting eliminated most of the population. In 1881, with the passage of the Saraiva Law, only 142,000 persons were permitted to vote, out of a population of approximately 15 million.[12] The country was effectively governed by a slave-supported oligarchy and a paternal chief of state. It was in some ways an artificial situation which only the Western Hemisphere could produce. Living in splendid isolation, the ruling class generally was able to ignore economic and social changes taking place in Europe and the United States.

Slowly the outside world caught up with Brazil. Changes began to creep into the country, and modern capitalism appeared after 1850. Coffee production brought about a complete realignment in the political and social structure that was to result eventually in the collapse of the empire. In the decade of the 1850's there was a final shift of political power from the old northeastern areas as the importance of the sugar, tobacco and cotton plantations, which had provided the wealth for the political structure, was overshadowed by the exploitation of coffee, a new money crop, and by planters in the south who did not rely on slave labor.

The slave trade, long under attack, finally began to decline. Although as early as 1827 the English and Brazilian governments signed a treaty declaring that after 1830 traffic in African slaves would be considered piracy, little was done by the Brazilians to stop the slave trade. Despite pressure from the English, the sugar plantation owners of the northeast continued to provide a market for slaves. In the 1840's over fifty thousand slaves a year were entering Brazil. The turning point came in the 1850's[13] as British patrol of the high seas became more exacting and the Brazilian government shifted its attitude and abolished the slave trade. After 1853, no more slaves were brought into Brazil.

Coffee production was in part responsible for this change of attitude of the Brazilian government. Coffee production had begun to boom in Brazil. Between 1851 and 1860, 27 million sacks were exported; from 1861 to 1870, 29 million sacks; from 1871 to 1880, 32.5 million sacks; and from 1881 to 1890, 51.6 million sacks.[14] Moreover, between 1850 and 1860, sixty-two industrial plants appeared, fourteen banking institutions, three savings banks, twenty steamship companies, eight mining companies, two gas companies and eight railroad companies. The impact of this type of commercial activity affected every phase of Brazilian life. Basically it meant that the sugar plantation owners were losing their undisputed control over the economic life of the nation.

During the 1850's foreign affairs in the La Plata area drew attention in Brazil. Clarence Haring offers an interesting and incisive approach by comparing Brazil's relationship to her La Plata area with the attitude of the United States toward the Caribbean.[15]

In 1851 and 1852 Brazil allied itself with Uruguayan elements to help overthrow domination of that country by Argentine dictator Juan Manuel Rosas. As a result, Brazilians played a positive role in Uruguayan politics for the next few years. From 1865 to 1870 Brazil formed an alliance with Uruguay and Argentina to fight against the expansionist plans of Paraguayan dictator Francisco Solano López. Brazil was the chief contributor of money and men to fight a war that dragged on for many years. The conflict ended in 1870 with the defeat of Paraguay, but Brazil suffered economically and from the loss of manpower.

The events of the war created a group of dissatisfied army men who were largely responsible for bringing the empire of Dom Pedro II to an end. The military after the Paraguayan war were convinced that they were not being given their fair share of the national budget or receiving the attention they should from the government. To counteract this situation and obtain a voice in national affairs, the army began to play politics and build up friends and spokesmen within the various political parties.

In 1870 a Republican party was organized by a group of citizens who sought to bring an end to the monarchy. Drawing heavily from the ranks of dissatisfied Liberal party politicians, the Republicans were able to take advantage of the resentment that had been building up against the political structure of Dom Pedro II. The antislavery struggle, the religious question and finally the military quarrels all became planks in the makeshift structure that the

Republican politicians were constructing.[16] A prominent figure in this movement was Professor Benjamin Constant Botelho de Magalhães, a leader of the younger military officers, who was convinced that military support would be the key to a successful revolution. In the state of Rio Grande do Sul younger political leaders such as Júlio de Castilhos and Joaquim Francisco de Assis Brasil also took up the banner of republicanism.

The collapse of the empire of Dom Pedro II can be further analyzed. Economics played an important role. The constantly growing power of the landholders in southern Brazil, who did not need nor approve the slavery and saw in the institution a drain of capital resources, was an important factor. Over the violent protests of the northeastern sugar planters, the Brazilian Parliament on May 13, 1888, abolished slavery and freed seven hundred thousand Negroes. Thus the Emperor lost the support of the wealthiest and most influential politicians of northeastern Brazil. In resentment, many of them began to look with sympathy at the republican movement.

The religious question further weakened the Emperor's position. Church support of Dom Pedro II faltered when he ordered the imprisonment of the bishops of Pernambuco and Pará in 1871. The tolerant attitude of Dom Pedro toward Masonic activity was in direct conflict with papal instructions to purge Masons from the Brazilian Church. When the bishops attacked the Masons from their pulpits, Dom Pedro ordered the bishops jailed. Shocked Church leaders began to re-think their unquestioned loyalty to Dom Pedro II. The Brazilian Church was in an uneasy position, since the leaders were in no way attracted to the Republican party, which was positivist in philosophy and not sympathetic to any close Church-State relationship. The Church in Brazil did not favor the downfall of the empire, but it did not give the Emperor the fervent support that it had previously.

Contributing further to the ultimate collapse of the Brazilian monarchy was Dom Pedro II's apparent lack of interest in forcing the continuation of the royal family on a reluctant nation. The aging monarch had no sons, and his daughter, Princess Isabel, in addition to having the reputation of a religious fanatic, was married to a Frenchman who was disliked by most Brazilian politicians. Republican leaders were able to focus a great deal of their attack on the monarchy by charging that Brazil's situation would be hopeless if and when Princess Isabel and her French husband assumed the throne.[17]

The small Brazilian entrepreneurial class also felt that their best interests were not being served by the political and economic policies of Dom Pedro II. A prominent industrialist, the Barão de Mauá (Irineu Evangelista de Souza), was in constant conflict with Dom Pedro II and his economic counselors.[18] Manipulation of the credit structure, granting of loans, concessions and special economic privileges to those favored by advisers to the Emperor, convinced many of the struggling entrepreneurs that a republic would provide a more equitable and honest government and promote the building of an effective economic structure.[19]

Next to collapse was the support of the military. Friction between the army and civilian ministers of war had been increasing since 1884. The army felt that the civilian cabinets were ignoring the military in their budgetary allotments. Younger army officers took public positions favoring abolition, and frequently clashed with cabinet ministers. The most prominent spokesman for the group was Marshal Manoel Deodoro da Fonseca. The crisis came to a head in mid-year 1889. On June 7, a new cabinet was formed to govern Brazil under the direction of a distinguished senator from Minas Gerais, Prime Minister Affonso Celso de Assis Figueiredo, Visconde de Ouro Prêto. Tighter controls over the military were expected, and tension mounted in Rio de Janeiro. On July 27, a crisis developed as the program of the new Ouro Prêto Ministry was rejected by the Chamber of Deputies in a 79 to 20 vote of no confidence. The Chamber was ordered dissolved and the interim Ouro Prêto Ministry governed until a new Chamber of Deputies, to be elected on November 20, 1889, could select a new cabinet.

On November 14, the Ouro Prêto Ministry, aware of army distrust of the government, ordered certain regiments suspected of disloyalty transferred to the interior of Brazil. The Ministry also called upon the Minister of Justice to mobilize the police force and the national guard for any eventuality. The regular army felt challenged and threatened by these moves.

Rumors began to flood the capital that Marshal Deodoro da Fonseca was to be imprisoned by the imperial government. Though personally loyal to the Emperor, Marshal Deodoro decided to

join the younger officers who favored an immediate revolution. When the Adjutant General of the Army, Marshal Floriano Peixoto, also sided with the revolutionaries, the success of the movement was guaranteed. At nine-thirty in the morning of November 15, 1889, the Visconde de Ouro Prêto and his aides were imprisoned by units of the Tenth Cavalry Division stationed in Rio de Janeiro. A military *coup d'état* had toppled the empire of Dom Pedro II. The aging monarch returned from his summer home in the mountains near Rio de Janeiro and, on November 17, 1889, left Brazil for exile.

Brazil entered a period of political transition with no bloodshed, no revolution and no mass participation. However, the population in the urban centers, both the elite and the small middle class, gave their general approval to the ending of the empire. Acceptance soon came from the provinces.

Chapter 2

The Old Republic: 1889 to 1930

The 1889 revolution is linked intimately with the events of 1930. The forceful entrance of the army into the political life of the republic marked the establishment and strengthening of a military caste that had been in decline since the Paraguayan War of 1865 to 1870. The first forty-one years of the republic, from 1889 to 1930, were strongly affected by the army, and the ultimate success of the 1930 revolution depended upon the action of the professional military.

The downfall of the Brazilian empire in 1889 was largely brought about by the military with the collaboration of a small but energetic group of Republican leaders.[1] Military control and influence in the central government resulted in the continuance of the absolutism of the monarch in the form of strong executive domination of the country. This did not mean arbitrary government. Any action taken by the central government was backed by constitutional provisions or sanctioned by the legislative branch of the government.

But the real base on which the new republic rested was a strong military clique supported by and allied with a small, tightly knit class of landowners, particularly as represented by the *fazendeiros*, owners of the large landed estates. After 1889 this group was dependent upon the army to preserve the status quo, and the fazendeiros rarely challenged the military. The army in turn identified itself with the small civilian element, which governed in the interests of its class and the military. Republican parties were formed in each state that accurately reflected this social oligarchy. Lawyers, physicians and engineers made up the majority of the politicians. Political positions were created for them; and it was on them that state politicians, in accord with the military, depended to guarantee satisfactory election results. "The party voters, in addition to those members of the machine, were multitudinous hangers-on who held small government jobs, either state or federal, merchants dependent for favors upon those in power, employees subject to pressure from employers, dependent artisans, and the friends of the local political chiefs. By force or fraud this body, numbering less than a million voters, was utilized by the machine to maintain themselves in office." [2]

But in the period 1889 to 1930, the problem was that 70 per cent of the Brazilians, the rural element, were almost totally excluded from voting on grounds of illiteracy. The reason for the depressed conditions of the average Brazilian was "the concentration of property and wealth, the relative absence of middle class groups in many regions, the concentration of the population, both rural and urban, in the unskilled labor categories and the ease with which a negative existence can be carried on." [3]

Regionalism constituted another problem facing the nation, and the struggle in 1930 was as much a regional battle as it was political and economic. Great differences in climate, race and cultural background created divergent political, social and economic conditions in the various sections of the country. Brazilians from one part of the immense country even today are startled by the differences they observe when they visit other states. The disparity in the distribution of the population and of wealth and the lack of effective communication among Brazil's twenty states led to an imbalance of political and economic power. The result, from 1889 to 1930, was a predominance of two Brazilian states, São Paulo and Minas Gerais, over the other eighteen. The political history of the old republic sharply reflected the regional imbalance created by the overwhelming power of these states.

Northern Brazil, for example, was forgotten and ignored by the central government. Despite the fact that more than 40 per cent of the national territory lies in northern Brazil, the region was sparsely populated and contributed little to the national economy.[4] Thus the states of northern Brazil scarcely participated in the Brazilian political scene, as a result of meager economic and political development and the lack of effective communication with other areas of the country. Rail and automobile road links to the south were non-existent so that the north was isolated from the rest of the country and could be reached only by ocean vessels and airplanes.

Northeastern Brazil to some degree faced the same problems as the north of the country. Communication with the more important south was also by sea or air, or haphazard transportation on the São Francisco River. Despite the economic importance it attained during the colonial period, the northeast in the twentieth century has been economically poor. A decadent agricultural system has limited the contribution of this region to the economic prosperity of the country.

Natives living in the backlands of the northeast are considered by many observers to be the best examples of the average Brazilian of the interior. A Brazilian historian, Pedro Calmon, describes their sentiments and political environment in the following manner: "Under the empire he considered himself governed by the King of Portugal; under the republic, he considered himself governed by the Emperor of Brazil. He throbs with old colonial sentiments; he repeats the resistance of fifteen generations of backwoods people. The fazendeiro is the spiritual chief of the clan, and continues to be called a 'major' or 'colonel,' as were the ancient officials of the ordinances, whose militarily administered governments left in the small communities pleasant memories that could not be erased. The priests have powers approximating those of the historic missionaries. Little is done without him and nothing is done against him."[5]

The plantation-owning families of the northeast had always been in control of the political structure and were unchallenged on the local level in pre-1930 Brazil. This was all that remained of the previous prestige of the planter aristocracy. However, the role of the northeast in the political affairs of the nation still had some importance. The cooperation of the states of Bahia and Pernambuco was sought by the political policy makers of São Paulo and Minas Gerais whenever disagreements occured over the choice of presidential candidates. To maintain political equilibrium the post of Vice-President was sometimes given to one of the larger northeastern states. The situation has been described as follows: "In Brazil there exist states that are leaders and those that are satellites. There are states of the first, second and third class. There are only two states of the first class, São Paulo and Minas Gerais. These supply the Presidents. The second-class states, Bahia, Pernambuco and Rio de Janeiro, may supply the Vice-Presidents. All the other states, with the exception of Rio Grande do Sul, form the third class."[6]

Below Bahia, the last of the northeastern states, was the economic heart of Brazil, dominated by São Paulo and Minas Gerais. Together the two states practically controlled the economic life of Brazil from the mid-nineteenth century to 1930. The economic power of the Paulistas, the inhabitants of the state of São Paulo, began in the 1850's, when coffee plantations in the *terra roxa*, or red-earth regions of the state, were developed. Heavy demand in the world market resulted in the early orientation of Brazilian economic life to the production and export of coffee. At the end of the empire in 1889 and throughout the period of the republic, the national financial structure rested almost exclusively on the revenue obtained from the export of coffee. Brazil supplied neary 70 per cent of the entire world production, and the state of São Paulo produced more than 70 per cent of Brazil's coffee.[7]

The 1891 Constitution permitted all states to make commercial treaties with foreign governments and to borrow money from foreign banking firms.[8] São Paulo took full advantage of these powers, adding to its economic power.

The standards of living in São Paulo were higher than in the north and northeast. The lines of communication in the state were comparatively well developed and connected with other economically important sections of the country.[9]

The state of Minas Gerais, bordering São Paulo, with its rich mineral deposits and considerable degree of agricultural diversification, was a natural ally of São Paulo. Minas Gerais also contributed extensively to the economic life of Brazil as a result of a balanced state economy. The pattern of settlement in the state was affected by the eighteenth-century "gold cycle," which attracted population from all parts of Brazil and Europe. The early development of effective communication with São Paulo and the south of Brazil aided the economic development of Minas Gerais.

Only one state challenged the wealth and dominance of São Paulo and Minas Gerais. Rio Grande do Sul, the southernmost state of Brazil, also wielded economic power in the years between 1889 and 1930, though not to the same degree as São Paulo and Minas Gerais. The development of the meat-packing industry after the First World War and agricultural diversification had brought economic progress and general prosperity to the region. These conditions, coupled wth regional antagonism, resulted in economic and political conflict with São Paulo and Minas Gerais. The leaders of Rio Grande do Sul resented the exclusive control of the national government by the two states.

Dominance over the national political structure was in part a reflection of Paulista and Mineiro economic power. It was also directly linked to the 1891 Constitution, which seemed to have been written exclusively for the wealthy states of southern Brazil. The Constitution declared that the President would be elected by direct popular vote, and the fact that more than 40 per cent of the nation's population was in the states of São Paulo, Minas Gerais and Rio de Janeiro further emphasized their power.[10]

Control of the executive office by São Paulo and Minas Gerais politicians was important, as the 1891 Constitution gave power to the President to intervene in the smaller, weaker states to "force upon them the rule of factions favored by the authorities in Rio de Janeiro [federal government] and the toleration of flagrantly unconstitutional acts by the state governments enjoying the favor of the national executive. The most serious charge that can be brought against the federalism established by the Constitution of 1891 has been the failure to satisfactorily adjust the relations of the states to the Federal government."[11] However, all interventions were carried out by the federal army in strict accordance with the dictates of the Constitution. There were no arbitrary or non-legal moves by the chief executive.

Though the first three civilian Presidents were natives of São Paulo (Prudente José de Morais e Barros, 1894–1898, Manuel Ferraz de Campos Sales, 1898–1902, Francisco de Paula Rodrigues Alves, 1902–1906), an early accord was reached between São Paulo and Minas Gerais which effectively blocked presidential candidates from the other states. However, no Paulista political leader occupied the executive office for the twenty-year period from 1906 to 1926.

The closest Rio Grande do Sul came to control of the national government during the old republic was in 1910. Gaúcho politicians took advantage of a temporary impasse between Minas Gerais and São Paulo politicians to dictate the official Republican party candidate for the 1910 presidential campaign. They chose a military man, though not a Gaúcho, Marshal Hermes da Fonseca, hoping that he would be more sympathetic to the state of Rio Grande do Sul than the previous Presidents. Minas Gerais and São Paulo Republican parties reluctantly went along with the decision.

Unexpected political opposition appeared when the country's leading statesman, Rui Barbosa, a native of the state of Bahia, threw his hat into the ring. An agitated race for the executive office developed as Barbosa ran as an independent and launched a vigorous attack on the military for their unquestioned and unqualified support of the political status quo.

The presidential struggle became known as a contest between *civilismo*, civilian government, and *cesarismo*, military government.[12] Though Rui Barbosa was very popular throughout the country, the professional politicians of Minas Gerais, São Paulo and Rio Grande do Sul realized that the political structure of the country depended upon the support of the military. Thus most state Republican party machines supported Hermes da Fonseca.

However, the vigorous campaign of Rui Barbosa, coupled with the disaffection of the various northeastern states, made it appear that the traditional army–Republican party control of the government was in danger. The power of the federal government and the military proved sufficient to elect Hermes da Fonseca. The Republican party controlled the electoral machinery in enough states, and though Rui Barbosa may have won in the streets he lost in the ballot boxes.[13] This was the first time that a candidate opposing the government machine was able to obtain a great percentage of the votes.[14] As a result of the agitated political campaign and the action of the northeastern states, President Hermes da Fonseca used the executive power to remove the political leaders who had supported Barbosa. Congressmen were not permitted to take their seats in the Brazilian Chamber of Deputies if the federal government felt they had been partisans of Rui Barbosa.

Federal coercion through the use of the army led to political rebellions in many states.[15] Though the rebellions were suppressed and political equilibrium maintained, there was bitter resentment against the national government on the part of the smaller states. When another agitated presidential election took place in 1930 which pitted three states against the national government, reprisals similar to those taken in 1910 led to revolution.[16]

Rio Grande do Sul's aspirations were not realized during the Hermes da Fonseca Administration, and another Minas Gerais politician, Venceslau Brás, was elected after a peaceful campaign in 1914. At the end of his term political arrangements were disrupted when the São Paulo presidential candidate, Rodrigues Alves, died shortly after winning the election. In the new election, the state of Rio Grande do Sul opposed the selection of any candidate from São Paulo or Minas Gerais. A political deadlock developed which was resolved only when Epitácio Pessôa, a native of the northeastern state of Paraíba, was chosen. At the time that Pessôa's name was announced to the public, he was attending the Versailles peace conference as one of the Brazilian delegates.[17]

Upon his return to Brazil, Epitácio Pessôa was elected with little opposition. President Pessôa understood that his choice as President was simply one of political compromise. He later wrote in his autobiography, *Pela verdade:* "I had never aspired to the presidency of the Republic. It was an idea that never bothered me, not because of any false modesty, nor because I believed I was incapable of managing the position, but due to the political organization of the country, which is set up in such a manner that the representatives of a small state like Paraíba could not honestly harbor such ambitions. Only the most unforeseen circumstances —such as the opposition of Rio Grande do Sul to any candidate from either São Paulo or Minas Gerais—and the fear that politicians from those states had of the candidacy of Rui Barbosa, were the reasons my name was chosen."[18]

Economic conditions faced by President Pessôa in 1919 were unfavorable. The postwar economic recession lowered the value of Brazilian currency, and the price of coffee declined. The great export balance accumulated during the war disappeared, and payments on foreign loans became due.[19] The Pessôa Administration moved immediately to save the coffee planters when the price of coffee dropped from twenty-three cents a pound in June, 1920, to nine cents a pound in January, 1921.[20] The federal government entered into a contract with the state of São Paulo, and a coffee program was instituted. This program provided federal government funds to buy surplus Brazilian coffee in the world market at high prices. The coffee would be stored by the government and later sold when world market prices rose. The Administration also negotiated a £5 million British loan in May, 1922, to finance the coffee program.[21]

President Pessôa's appointment of civilians to the posts of Minister of the Army and Minister of the Navy created another crisis in Brazilian political circles.[22] Many military officials resented this action and expressed dissatisfaction by opposing the official Republican party presidential candidate in the 1922 election. They felt that the best interests of the army were no longer being served by the Republican party and that a President should be elected who would be more sympathetic to the army and navy. Army men opposing the Republican party in 1922 received open support from dissident political groups in the states of Rio Grande do Sul, Bahia and Rio de Janeiro. It appears that the action of these states was more an attempt to break the exclusive control of São Paulo and Minas Gerais than to support the military, who had no clear political program.

The official São Paulo–Minas Gerais Republican party candidate was the governor of Minas Gerais, Artur da Silva Bernardes. The military and dissenting states favored Nilo Peçanha, a former Vice-President and popular political leader from the state of Rio de Janeiro.[23] Though the 1922 presidential campaign was agitated, the strength of São Paulo and Minas Gerais was sufficient to secure a victory over the dissatisfied military and the smaller states, and thus preserve the traditional political equilibrium. The domination of the state electoral machinery in São Paulo, Minas Gerais and a majority of the other states was sufficient to assure an overwhelming victory for Bernardes in the balloting. The situation was so tense, however, that the retiring chief executive, President Pessôa, declared that he believed President-elect Bernardes would not be able to remain twenty-four hours in the presidential palace.[24] Nevertheless, despite agitated political and military conditions, President Bernardes purged the political opposition in Bahia, Rio de Janeiro and Pernambuco during his four-year term of office.

Growing dissatisfaction between some elements of the military caste and the federal government after the election led to an armed rebellion.[25] In July, 1922, units of the federal military garrison stationed in Rio de Janeiro, the national capital, revolted and called upon the citizens to fight the federal government.[26] Though the rebellion stemmed in part from a sincere desire of the younger officers to break the control of the Republican party of São Paulo and Minas Gerais, it also indicated that the identification of the military caste with the federal government was weakening.[27] The lack of political manifestos or proclamations and the failure of other garrisons to join the revolt, resulted in the defeat of the movement.[28] A small unit of officers and men in the Fort Copacabana Garrison in Rio de Janeiro gained national fame when they refused to surrender, and attacked several thousand loyal federal troops. Discontent within the army caste against the traditional political equilibrium was developing.

As political tension and military opposition to the Bernardes regime continued, Bernardes requested and received "state of siege" powers from Congress, and Brazil was governed for nearly four years in this manner. In July, 1924, another small armed rebellion occurred. The outbreak centered in São Paulo and Rio Grande do Sul and, like the 1922 movement, failed to win over top military figures; nor did the São Paulo population support the rebellion.[29] Though the garrison in São Paulo was forced to surrender the capital to loyal federal troops, one group refused to capitulate and fought their way south to the state of Rio Grande do Sul. General Isidoro Lopes was in charge of the rebel group, which was later divided into three commands: one under Lieutenant Newton Estilac Leal, one under Colonel Miguel Costa and a third under Captain Juarez Távora.[30]

In October, 1924, another series of uprisings against the government took place in Rio Grande do Sul. Federal units in Uruguaiana, São Borja, São Luís and Alegrete, where Lieutenant João Alberto Lins de Barros was in command, went into rebellion. In Santo Ângelo, in Rio Grande do Sul, Captain Luís Carlos Prestes joined the rebelling units and issued a manifesto, which declared: "the whole of Brazil from north to south ardently desire, deep in their conscience, the victory of the revolutionaries, because they want the peoples' vote to be secret, because they want the wishes of the people respected in the polling places, because they want the confiscation of the great fortunes made by members of the government through the use of public money, because they want the government to be less political and more interested in helping the people." The manifesto contained many confused and disconnected ideas and ended by stating: "Today, October 29, by orders of General Isidoro, Gaúcho revolutionary forces are in rebellion; today revolutionary chiefs, Honório Lemes and Zéca Neto have entered the state, according to an organized grand plan. In this manner, from this communion of the army and the people, with nationals and foreigners, a rapid end of the armed struggle in Brazil will occur." [31] There was no response from the public.

In March, 1925, the Rio Grande do Sul rebels linked up with the unsuccessful São Paulo rebels of General Isidoro. Prestes took over-all command; Lieutenants Osvaldo Cordeiro de Faria, Siqueira Campos, João Alberto Lins de Barros and Djalma Dutra were placed in command of the four divisions of the column.[32] For nearly three years the "Prestes column," as it came to be known, operating in the backlands of Brazil, was attacked constantly by federal troops, but remained undefeated. The rebel column marched more than fifteen thousand miles and harassed the government militarily and politically.[33] The leaders of the military column, no longer associated with the traditional army caste, advocated land reform and better economic conditions for the rural and urban workers. Soon the lieutenants gained great popularity among the lower classes, and Luís Carlos Prestes became known as the Cavaleiro da Esperança (Knight of Hope).

In 1926, at the close of the Bernardes regime, it was estimated that more than $100 million had been spent by the federal government in attempts to destroy the column.[34] In 1927 the column disbanded and went into exile when the government forces, under the direction of Major Pedro Aurélio Góes Monteiro, organized hand-picked armed bands, *grupos de caça,* who were deputized into the federal army, given arms and uniforms, and told to attack the column. They did so successfully. The government was using the same tactics against the column that the column had used against the government.[35] However, there was an ever-growing body of younger, disenchanted military men who sympathized with the army officers in exile and created a potentially dangerous situation. When the Rio Grande do Sul rebellion began in October, 1930, many of the revolutionary army officers were the *Tenente* veterans of the 1922 and 1924 campaigns against the government.

A factor of economic importance during the Bernardes regime was the President's open hostility to federal financial aid for the coffee producers of São Paulo. In 1924 the stabilization of the price of coffee was removed from federal control. The problem of the purchase of surplus coffee was turned over to the state of São Paulo.[36]

There was little protest from the Paulistas, for the general economic prosperity of the period enabled the state of São Paulo to finance the purchase of the surplus coffee. The Bernardes regime drew to a close in 1926 in calmer political conditions than those in which it began. The financial structure of Brazil, although oriented almost entirely to the export of coffee, appeared to be on a sound economic foundation as a result of high prices in the world market.

The 1926 presidential election of Washington Luís Pereira de Souza, governor of São Paulo, continued the traditional political equilibrium. Minas Gerais and São Paulo continued to dominate the national political scene. However, despite the lack of organized political and military opposition to the Paulista President, the Washington Luís Administration was to end in revolution four years later.

When Washington Luís assumed office, the prosperous years from 1926 to 1928 concealed the basic weakness of the Brazilian economic structure, its reliance on export revenues from a single crop. Early in his administration, Washington Luís appointed Getúlio Vargas, a Rio Grande do Sul congressional leader, to the post of Minister of Finance.[37] Vargas inaugurated the Washington Luís program of monetary reform and currency stabilization. The Brazilian mil-réis was stabilized at twelve cents, and a stabilization bureau was created to insure the conversion of notes into gold at a fixed rate of exchange. The Bank of Brazil was authorized to buy and sell foreign exchange and to maintain the mil-réis at a fixed rate. As a result of these measures the mil-réis remained stable until the New York Stock Market crash of October, 1929.[38] The financial program of the President became an important factor in the downfall of the national government when the world economic crisis occurred in 1929.

In 1928, when preparations for the 1930 presidential elections began, the political relations of the federal government with the state of Rio Grande do Sul were excellent. Getúlio Vargas, after an undistinguished record as Finance Minister, was recalled to Rio Grande do Sul by Antônio Augusto Borges de Medeiros, political boss of the state. Vargas was selected as candidate for governor and won an easy victory in 1928.[39]

Rio Grande do Sul received extra financial aid, which was reflected in economic progress for the state. The *xarque,* or dried meat, industry was expanded, agricultural experiment stations were installed, ocean ports were modernized and road facilities were improved.

It appeared that a new era had begun in Brazilian political affairs. The federal government, normally supported by the Republican parties of São Paulo and Minas Gerais, was now, for the first time in many years, bolstered by Rio Grande do Sul. The military establishment seemed content to continue the political status quo oriented around the major states of the nation. Political equilibrium of the country seemed secure. Yet seven months after the March, 1930, elections there occurred the first successful revolution in the history of the Republic of Brazil.

Chapter 3

The Politicians and the 1930 Revolution

Political leaders in Brazil seemed relaxed in 1928 as the Washington Luís Administration passed the halfway mark in an unaccustomed atmosphere of domestic peace and tranquility. Antônio Carlos Ribeiro de Andrada, governor of Minas Gerais and chief of the state Republican party, in accordance with tradition and previous agreements expected the support of President Washington Luís and the state of São Paulo in his candidacy for the presidential office. Governor Antônio Carlos had little reason to believe that he would not be selected as the 1930 presidential candidate. His Republican party had supported Paulista politicians in 1926 when they selected Governor Washington Luís for the presidency, and he expected São Paulo Republican party support in 1930 when he would make his bid for the office.

However, there were indications that Antônio Carlos faced strong federal and state opposition in his desire to attain the presidential office. Part of the opposition on the state level stemmed from a bill the governor had forced through the state legislature that made religious instruction mandatory in state-controlled schools.[1] Some elements felt that Antônio Carlos was too militant a Catholic and out of step with the prevailing attitude toward religion. Thus the law had resulted in political protests in Minas Gerais and other parts of Brazil. Antônio Carlos was not supported by the politically powerful Masonic order, because of his close association with the Catholic element in Minas Gerais.[2]

On the national level, President Washington Luís personally considered Antônio Carlos incompetent. In 1928 there were indications that Washington Luís might not continue the tradition of alternating the presidential office between São Paulo and Minas Gerais. Voluminous praise of Júlio Prestes, governor of São Paulo, began to appear in newspapers favorable to the government. Early in 1929 rumors indicated that the President was going to back Prestes in the next presidential election.[3] The scene was now set for a break in the traditional Minas Gerais–São Paulo arrangement of presidential succession. Washington Luís,[4] of course, had the support of the São Paulo Republican party. Also, in December, 1928, Governor Getúlio Vargas offered the complete cooperation of Rio Grande do Sul in the question of presidential succession.[5] Thus the first move was made by the man who was to hold the center of the Brazilian political stage from 1930 to 1954.

Getúlio Dorneles Vargas was complicated, devious and superbly political. He has never been described or written about in terms that completely satisfy his friends or his enemies. There were too many sides to Getúlio Vargas. No one "true" picture of the man will ever emerge. Thus the simple question, what manner of man was the future political leader of Brazil, is a difficult one to answer.

Vargas was born on April 19, 1883, in São Borja in the southern state of Rio Grande do Sul, and grew up on a ranch near the Argentine border. Growing up in the state of Rio Grande do Sul implies a great deal. The Gaúcho differs in personality from his fellow countrymen. The citizen of Rio Grande do Sul is first a Gaúcho and second a Brazilian. The blame is not his alone. Rio Grande do Sul was land that was fought over. Too many nations and too many people were interested in the rich farmland close to the La Plata Basin, and often there were more soldiers than settlers in the territory. Throughout the colonial period Spaniards and Indians attacked the Portuguese colonists. Settlers in Rio Grande do Sul lived with rifles at their sides.

Brazilians forged in this environment did not have the same approach to politics as those in the central or northern areas of the country. Political questions in Rio Grande do Sul were often resolved by armed force. There was little compromise. The dominant

Republican party of Rio Grande do Sul had defeated the Federalists. This was a political fact of life.

Rio Grande do Sul was dominated for fourteen years by Júlio Castilhos, Republican party leader, whose death in 1903 did not interrupt the strong positivist influence he had brought into the affairs of the former province. The "14th of July" state constitution of Rio Grande do Sul differed from other state constitutions. More centralized, it contained three cardinal points which always left an uneasiness in the São Paulo–Minas Gerais–oriented federal government. They concerned the constitutionality and the possibility of conflict between the federal Constitution and the Gaúcho state document. The three major points were: First, the function of the state legislature was reduced to that of budgetary supervision; second, legislative initiative was in the hands of the chief executive through the manipulation of popular referendums; third, the indefinite re-election of the governor of the state was permitted as long as three-quarters of all the votes were obtained by the candidate.[6] The Rio Grande do Sul constitution created a strong centralized power structure in the hands of the executive branch of the state government. Borges de Medeiros inherited the post of Júlio de Castilhos in 1903 and continued the political pattern of his predecessor.

The political mold of Rio Grande do Sul had left its imprint clearly on Getúlio Vargas' father, General Manuel do Nascimento Vargas, who was a perfect product of the land. Of Azorian descent, a tough rancher, General Vargas was the local political boss of the frontier-border town of São Borja.[7] General Vargas earned his titles in the many armed political struggles fought in the state of Rio Grande do Sul.

Getúlio Vargas wanted a military career like his father's, and he was sent first, along with two brothers, to the military school of Ouro Prêto, Minas Gerais. Within a short time, however, a student brawl resulted in the death of one of the cadets, and the three Vargas boys returned home. Vargas went next to military school at Rio Pardo in Rio Grande do Sul and remained there about a year until another student rebellion impelled him to withdraw.[8] He was later forced to serve out the regular term of compulsory military service as a private in the Twenty-fifth Infantry Battalion, stationed in Pôrto Alegre. In 1902 a border dispute between Bolivia and

Brazil threatened peaceful relations between the two nations. The Brazilian army was mobilized for action in the Acre Territory. Getúlio Vargas accompanied the Twenty-fifth Infantry Battalion to the frontier town of Corumbá in Mato Grosso. Apparently Vargas found the experience so disagreeable that it ended once and for all any plans that he had for a military career.

Getúlio Vargas' next move was to matriculate in the law school of Pôrto Alegre. Law schools in Brazil, as in much of Latin America, are the traditional training ground for politicians. The students are drawn from the upper middle class, and form the cadre of the political structure. While Vargas was in law school he became acquainted with many students who later became important politicians in Rio Grande do Sul and accompanied Vargas when he went to Rio de Janeiro in 1930. The law school was involved in the question of the gubernatorial succession in the state of Rio Grande do Sul and most students were Republican party members, supporting Borges de Medeiros. Vargas and other students participated in breaking up a political rally of the opposition by firing shots over the heads of the audience. Vargas, questioned many years later concerning the incident, is reported to have replied: "That was the only way to break up that meeting." [9]

Upon his graduation from law school in 1909 two choices were open to him. He was offered an instructorship at the law school or the chance of serving as a district attorney for the state in Pôrto Alegre. Selecting the district attorney post, he gained invaluable experience in dealing with people in the lower income groups. The isolation of the political elite from the problems of the working class is often so deep that it can never be bridged. Vargas was able to take advantage of this experience in his later political career.

Shortly after he assumed the post of district attorney he married fifteen-year-old Darcí Sarmanho, the daughter of a rancher and successful businessman from São Borja. He received a large tract of land from his father, and was thus able to supplement his meager political salary and survive the lean years of his apprenticeship in politics.

After working less than a year as district attorney he was given an opportunity to serve in the state legislature. Vargas obtained the post as a result of the prestige of his father in Republican party political circles. São Borja was Republican political territory and

Barry College Library
Miami, Florida

General Manuel Vargas controlled the local electoral machinery. An opening occurred in the state assembly and Vargas was "elected." He served from 1909 to 1913. A personal dispute between General Vargas and leaders of the Republican party led to Getúlio's resignation and return to São Borja, where he entered private law practice.[10] Nearly four years elapsed before the Vargas clan made peace with the chief of the state Republican party. During this period Vargas was approached by former colleagues and offered the post of police chief of Pôrto Alegre. He refused the offer and remained at home in São Borja.

In 1916 the central Republican party established harmony with General Vargas, and Getúlio Vargas once more took his place in the state assembly as Republican party representative from São Borja to serve from 1917 to 1922. Vargas was a skillful parliamentarian, and was soon chosen majority leader.[11]

Borges de Medeiros decided in 1922 that Vargas should run for the national Congress as the Republican party candidate. He was unopposed, and thus began his career on the national level, at the age of thirty-nine. Just as Vargas was leaving for Rio de Janeiro, an armed political revolt broke out in Rio Grande do Sul between Republican forces and Federalist politicians led by Joaquim Francisco de Assis Brasil. The rebellion was incited by the re-election of Borges de Medeiros as governor of Rio Grande do Sul for his fifth consecutive term, which would run from 1923 to 1928. Borges de Medeiros had been continuously elected since 1903 and his Federalist opponents felt the only way out of this impasse was to field an army. Republican forces were mobilized to meet the threat, and Getúlio Vargas was given the temporary rank of colonel. He also received orders to organize a citizens' cavalry unit from São Borja. The military objective of his unit was to free the neighboring town of Itaqui, where a fellow politician, Osvaldo Aranha, was besieged by Federalist forces. En route Vargas was ordered to turn over his command of the Seventh Provisional Auxiliary Corps to his cousin Deoclécio Dorneles Mota, as Vargas' election to the federal Congress made active military service unconstitutional.

Vargas, upon taking his seat in the federal Congress in 1923, immediately made clear the position of the Rio Grande do Sul Republican party in relation to the revolution being waged in his state. The young congressman warned the federal government not to intervene and stated that "Rio Grande do Sul desires the right to be governed by men of their own choosing and laws of their own making within a constitutional framework." [12] The position of Rio Grande do Sul Republican party politicians in the federal Congress was a delicate one, as they had supported the opposition candidate for the presidency in the agitated 1922 contest. Artur da Silva Bernardes, President of Brazil from 1922 to 1926, did not look with particular favor on Rio Grande do Sul, but Vargas apparently succeeded in re-establishing good relations between the federal government and his state.

Events in Rio Grande do Sul also helped Vargas when a truce in the armed struggle was reached in December, 1923. The federal government played an important part in the Treaty of Pedras Altas, which ended the war between the Republicans and the Federalists in Rio Grande do Sul.[13]

One of the most significant points of the settlement had a direct effect on the future of Congressman Vargas. This was the clause that stated that the governor of the state was no longer eligible for re-election. Vargas was to be the first and last beneficiary of this clause. Also, the federal government would assist in the supervision of elections.

Getúlio Vargas served in the federal Congress in the years 1923 to 1927. At the time of the 1924 military rebellion in São Paulo, he went on record as opposing the armed revolt and accused the opposition political party in Rio Grande do Sul of attempting to take advantage of the unsettled political climate to harass the Republican party. During the period that Vargas served in the Chamber of Deputies he was an unimportant member of its Finance Committee.[14]

Brazilian politics in 1926 was peaceful from north to south, in contrast to previous years. The choice of the official government candidate, Washington Luís, was accepted by every state, including normally suspicious and combative Rio Grande do Sul. That peace had been made between the state Republican forces of Rio Grande do Sul and the national government is indicated by the nearly 100,000 votes that Washington Luís received in that state, in contrast to the 1924 elections when the Gaúcho Republican machine delivered nearly 96,000 votes to the opposition candidate.[15] Borges de Medeiros had come to terms with the federal government after nearly a quarter of a century of struggle. Soon results were seen in the national government.

President Washington Luís told Borges de Medeiros that he wanted someone from Rio Grande do Sul to serve as his Finance Minister and preferred Getúlio Vargas over any other possible candidate. Borges de Medeiros informed Vargas of the request and indicated that he was pleased with the appointment. Repercussions in the state of Rio Grande do Sul were extremely favorable. According to many contemporary observers, though Vargas had served on the Finance Committee of the Chamber of Deputies, the Gaúcho politician most qualified for the post was Lindolfo Color. However, Washington Luís was determined to have Getúlio Vargas in that post.[16] It has been suggested that Washington Luís had a financial program that was so well developed and detailed in its planning that the autocratic President simply did not want any interference from a determined and well-informed technician. Vargas accepted the position and in methodical fashion set out to learn something about the nation's finances. One of the techniques used by Vargas was to permit people who had complaints and requests to visit the Minister of Finance once a week. Long lines of citizens gathered outside his office, waiting patiently to speak to him, and Vargas listened carefully to each one, speaking very little himself.

Though he served as Minister of Finance for about a year, approximately six months after he accepted the post he was abruptly informed that he would be a candidate for governor of the state of Rio Grande do Sul. He would replace Borges de Medeiros, who was apparently willing to step down for the period 1928 to 1933 after having controlled the state tightly for twenty-five years. The 1924 political treaty of Pedras Altas was being honored.

Borges de Medeiros circulated an explanation of his actions to the various Republican clubs of Rio Grande do Sul, stating: "It is necessary to maintain political and administrative continuity, which has been the most notable characterstic of the government of Rio Grande do Sul and the most solid guarantee of order and progress." [17] Getúlio Vargas, speaking a short time later in Pôrto Alegre, took special pains to inform the press and political observers that his choice had been dictated by Borges de Medeiros and no pressure had been applied by President Washington Luís.

Offered a farewell banquet by the President of the republic,

Vargas toasted the President by saying: "When I accepted the position of Finance Minister, I had your excellency as my chief, a person worthy of all the praise I had heard, but you were an unknown quantity to me. In the year we have worked together in public affairs this man who was my chief changed without my realizing it into a teacher and a friend. Rio Grande do Sul will support with enthusiasm the government of your excellency which has been so rich in accomplishments and has even greater hopes for the future." [18]

In the November, 1927, state elections Getúlio Vargas won an unopposed contest for the governorship of Rio Grande do Sul. Vargas was to govern for only two years, 1928 to 1930. The accomplishments of those two years are interesting and give some clues to his later actions. Borges de Medeiros permitted the cautious Vargas to shape his own approach to politics.

One of Vargas' first moves was his treatment of the political opposition in the municipal elections in the state which took place shortly after he assumed office. Elections were held in an atmosphere of tolerance and were the closest to free elections of any ever recorded in Rio Grande do Sul history. Before Vargas took office, opposition to the dominant Republican party was barely tolerated. A common expression describing the political atmosphere was "For the party faithful—everything; for the uninterested—simply the law; for the opposition—not even water." [19] Vargas apparently changed this, and in the counting of votes where the results were not clear, Vargas permitted the opposition to gain a few new seats in the state assembly. The old politicians looked with some suspicion at these tactics, whereas the opposition felt that a new era had dawned in Rio Grande do Sul politics.

Getúlio Vargas as governor had approximately two years of prosperity before the world economic crisis closed in on Brazil. The two years were profitable ones for the state. Vargas was influential in assisting the aviation industry to get a start in Rio Grande do Sul, and the state became one of the heaviest investors in Varig airlines. Agriculture was also encouraged in an effort to tear the Gaúcho away from economic dependence on cattle raising. The cultivation of wheat and grapes was encouraged. Special credit facilities were set up for cattle and pork producers, and they were urged to set up their own packing facilities so that they could export to other areas of Brazil and to foreign countries. Suggestions by the governor also resulted in the expansion of the coal industry.

The picture of Getúlio Vargas up to 1930 is almost complete. Few changes or surprises were seen in the next twenty-four years that were not revealed in this formative period. Vargas was conditioned and trained to practically every level of political experience in Brazil. Pragmatic and unromantic concerning the political process, Vargas appeared to hold few illusions about the body politic in Brazil. He had been groomed in a political atmosphere that understood the use of power. In the Vargas approach, men in executive power were expected to use their offices to improve the lot of the people. They were expected to help the economic development of the state. There were no forbidden social areas for the government.

Getúlio Vargas worked hard and long at the business of politics and was adept in performance. His law background, his experience in the state legislature, his training in the national Congress and finally his cabinet appointment gave him a tremendous breadth of experience in Brazilian political affairs. His crowning achievement up to this point had been his selection as the successor to Borges de Medeiros. As one surveys the possible candidates for that position among the bright young politicians who were available in Rio Grande do Sul, including such men as João Neves da Fontoura, Lindolfo Color and Osvaldo Aranha, it becomes apparent that Borges de Medeiros was exceptionally skilled and perceptive in assessing the political potential of Getúlio Vargas. President Washington Luís shrewdly noted once that "Vargas' friends always seemed to force him in the direction he originally planned to go." [20]

A new and surprising aspect of Vargas' was his ability to conspire quietly. This uncanny ability to move in several directions at the same time came to light in the period preceding the presidential elections and was perfected during the fifteen years he remained as dictator of Brazil.

None of this was clear in 1928. At that time Washington Luís was not expected to have any trouble in electing another Paulista to the presidency, in spite of protests from the governor of Minas Gerais.

Antônio Carlos Ribeiro de Andrada was aware that Washington Luís was preparing Júlio Prestes for the Presidency. Washington Luís, in breaking with tradition, had allied the Administration with

São Paulo, Rio Grande do Sul and seventeen other Brazilian states to make certain that Júlio Prestes would be the next President. Apparently Governor Antônio Carlos decided that if he could not be President he would at least block the Paulista candidate. However, Minas Gerais, acting alone, was too weak to stop the presidential plans of the federal government. To prevent Júlio Prestes from attaining the presidency it would be necessary for Minas Gerais politicians to secure the cooperation of Rio Grande do Sul.

The first positive move toward the arrangement was a letter from Antônio Carlos to Governor Getúlio Vargas in January, 1929, in which he declared that the Minas Gerais Republican party would not, under any circumstances, accept Júlio Prestes. He went on to intimate that the best method of combating Washington Luís would be to enter a Gaúcho candidate supported unanimously by Minas Gerais and Rio Grande do Sul. Antônio Carlos declared: "The combination of Minas Gerais and Rio Grande do Sul would result in a much more representative person than one chosen simply by the chief executive." [21]

Governor Vargas replied, noting the amicable relations existing between Minas Gerais and Rio Grande do Sul. He declared that his state had not committed itself on the question of presidential succession. Vargas also informed Antônio Carlos that he was interested in the future plans of the Minas Gerais governor. At the same time that Antônio Carlos was corresponding with Getúlio Vargas, he was attempting to reach an agreement with President Washington Luís concerning the question of presidential succession. He was rebuffed by the chief executive, who refused to discuss the question.

In May, 1929, both Antônio Carlos and Getúlio Vargas wrote letters to President Washington Luís offering their full cooperation with whatever action the President felt necessary regarding the March, 1930, election. On May 10, 1929, Vargas wrote: "Your Excellency can remain tranquil that the Republican party of Rio Grande do Sul will not fail with its support at the necessary moment." [22] Vargas also stated that the question of public debate concerning the presidential succession should begin only when Washington Luís felt it was opportune.

A week after the Vargas letter, Minas Gerais politicians once again suggested the possibility of combined action by Minas Gerais and Rio Grande do Sul to present a Gaúcho candidate for the presidency. Vargas refused to act upon the suggestion, as wide publicity had been given to the letter written by Antônio Carlos to Washington Luís. Antônio Carlos had agreed that the time was not right to discuss the problem of presidential succession. President Washington Luís, pleased with such demonstrations of cooperation from Minas Gerais and Rio Grande do Sul, declared that any public debate on the question of presidential succession would be premature before the month of September, 1929. At the same time, the President, as well as official government publications responding to official pressure, continued to praise Júlio Prestes. These obvious manifestations served to orient the smaller states to the unofficially favored candidate of the federal government.

Although political peace seemed possible to Washington Luís, two weeks later, on June 17, 1929, a daring and audacious agreement was made in Rio de Janeiro proposing the name of Getúlio Vargas for the presidency of the nation. Gaúcho Congressman João Neves da Fontoura, a close personal friend of Vargas' and the dynamic leader of the Rio Grande do Sul congressional bloc, acted on his own initiative and signed the pact without consulting other Rio Grande do Sul politicians. Apparently he felt that the opportunity to project a Gaúcho into the executive office was too important to let slip by. In contrast to the action of João Neves, the Minas Gerais representatives acted only on direct orders from Antônio Carlos. The main terms of the pact centered on an agreement between the political leaders of Minas Gerais and Rio Grande do Sul to present the name of a Gaúcho for the presidential office. The name of the Rio Grande do Sul candidate would be either Borges de Medeiros or Getúlio Vargas. As there was some fear that Washington Luís might attempt to split the Minas Gerais–Rio Grande do Sul alliance by accepting a compromise candidate from Minas Gerais, it was further agreed that this would be acceptable only if the vice-presidency was reserved for Rio Grande do Sul. Until Borges de Medeiros signed the agreement it was to be considered only as a preliminary understanding.[23]

After the accord was signed a few days later in Minas Gerais by Antônio Carlos it was sent to Rio Grande do Sul, where Borges de Medeiros approved the unauthorized action by João Neves enthusiastically and declared: "We should not and cannot refuse the agreement that Minas Gerais has offered."[24] At the same time, Borges de Medeiros declined the offer to be the presidential candidate. Getúlio Vargas was much less enthusiastic. Vargas had maneuvered Rio Grande do Sul into an excellent bargaining position. No matter what the result of the battle for the presidency, Vargas and the state of Rio Grande do Sul would benefit. Vargas had convinced Washington Luís that Rio Grande do Sul would cooperate with the federal government. As a result of the pact approved by Borges de Medeiros, however, it appeared that Vargas would have to oppose President Washington Luís. The signature of Borges de Medeiros upon the pact left no other action possible for the governor. Vargas delayed as long as possible. The chief of the Republican party in Rio Grande do Sul counseled Vargas that he would run no risk in attempting the Minas Gerais proposal. He informed Vargas that even if Washington Luís were to refuse his candidacy, the President would probably substitute a compromise candidate. At the end of June, Vargas accepted.

Vargas explained his position in a letter to Washington Luís on July 11, 1929. The letter contained a statement that the Minas Gerais proposal to submit Vargas' name for the presidency had been presented to Borges de Medeiros, who had accepted for him. Also, Borges de Medeiros had suggested that the proposal be submitted first for approval to President Washington Luís. Vargas took advantage of the fact that Washington Luís had not officially announced his decision to support Júlio Prestes. Vargas wrote: "Since you have not indicated your preference for any one candidate this will not compromise you in any way." The letter continued, "Your Excellency need have no fear that I will withdraw support from your financial program."[25]

The Rio Grande do Sul politician José Antônio Flôres da Cunha, who delivered this letter to the President, later wrote: "Washington looked like a man who had fallen from a skyscraper."[26] The President was reported to have declared: "This can't be. I have just received reassuring correspondence from Vargas."[27] On July 20 the governor of Minas Gerais sent a letter to Washing Luís stating: "Minas Gerais supports the candidacy of Getúlio Vargas, who, as former Cabinet Minister and Governor of Rio Grande do Sul, should have the firm support of your Administration."[28] President Washington Luís answered this letter verbally, saying that he would get in touch with the political leaders of the other states with regard to the question. Reports concerning this development began to appear in the Rio de Janeiro press but were denied by the federal government.

Washington Luís then dispatched telegrams to eighteen state governors of Brazil requesting that they support Júlio Prestes for the presidency. Washington Luís failed to mention the name of Getúlio Vargas. All states, with the exception of one, indicated they would support Júlio Prestes for the presidency. The northeastern state of Paraíba refused. Paraíba's decision to ignore the Administration was a result of the acceptance by its governor, João Pessôa, of the vice-presidency on the Vargas slate. His terse rejection of Júlio Prestes' candidacy, "Nego (I refuse)," became a rallying cry of the opponents of the federal government.

With seventeen of the twenty states cooperating with the Administration, Washington Luís informed Vargas by letter on July 26, 1929, "Other states have indicated that they have accepted another name equally dignified, equally cooperative with the present government, Dr. Júlio Prestes. There do not exist any motives to refuse the request of the state delegates." [29] In the same letter Washington Luís repeated sections of Vargas' letter of May 10 referring to the cooperation that could be expected from Rio Grande do Sul. Washington Luís sent a similar letter to Antônio Carlos. The determined action of President Washington Luís to support his candidate surprised most of the politicians from Minas Gerais and Rio Grande do Sul, who favored the alliance between the two states. It had been expected that Washington Luís would pick a third person who would serve as a compromise candidate in order to avoid a bitter political battle. When it was certain that the federal government was going to back Júlio Prestes, Rio Grande do Sul politicians were placed in a difficult position.

Vargas, seeing the development of this situation, wrote immediately to Washington Luís and declared that he was prepared to withdraw his candidacy. To further disentangle himself, Vargas turned to his secretary of the interior, Osvaldo Aranha, a charismatic and flamboyant figure who was also a long-time personal friend. Aranha was sent to Rio de Janeiro to arrange an understanding with Washington Luís. He failed and telegraphed Vargas, "We are politically abandoned. The only thing left is a dignified accord or a brave battle. Choose one and give me your orders."[30] While Vargas was seeking a way out of the commitment to run for president, the Republican party of Minas Gerais voted unanimously to support his candidacy. On August 1 Antônio Carlos informed Washington Luís in a letter: "It is impossible to agree with your choice of Júlio Prestes." In addition, he informed the President that Paraíba, Minas Gerais and Rio Grande do Sul were officially backing the candidacy of Getúlio Vargas and João Pessôa.[31] The political accord of these three states became known as the Liberal Alliance.[32] In August the federal government officially announced that it was supporting Júlio Prestes for the presidency.

On August 5, 1929, the political campaign was opened in the national Congress by João Neves. From this date the Congress was almost completely taken up with campaign speeches for the Liberal Alliance or for Júlio Prestes. In early September a Liberal Alliance convention met in Rio de Janeiro and officially nominated Getúlio Vargas and João Pessôa. Despite popular acclaim all over the country, Vargas knew that with only Paraíba it would be impossible for the Minas Gerais–Rio Grande do Sul coalition to win the election. Vargas therefore continued his efforts throughout the months of August and September to come to a peaceful understanding with President Washington Luís and Júlio Prestes. Early in September, Vargas tried to obtain the services of former President Epitácio Pessôa as an agent of conciliation, but Washington Luís refused to discuss the question. At the same time the platforms of both candidates were made public. With the exception of the request for amnesty for the revolutionaries of 1922 and 1924 favored by the Liberal Alliance, the programs were basically identical.

In October, 1929, six months before the election, Vargas saw an opportunity to come to terms with the Administration. A division in the Minas Gerais Republican party occurred over the choice for the next governor of that state. Governor Antônio Carlos had approved a candidate whom the Vice-President of Brazil, a Mineiro, refused to support. The significance of a strong splinter group in the normally unified Republican party of Minas Gerais meant less votes for Vargas and he appeared determined to get out of the campaign. Vargas met with Borges de Medeiros and Osvaldo Aranha in November, 1929, and a decision was made to send Senator Firmino Paim Filho to confer with Washington Luis and Júlio Prestes.

Vargas advised the senator: "There are only two possibilities in the March elections—a defeat and the subsequent submission to the victor, or a revolutionary protest of uncertain consequences of victory, but certain to ruin the country."[33] Vargas, with the approval of Borges de Medeiros, stated that if the São Paulo governor agreed with the ideas of the Liberal Alliance, it would not be necessary for Rio Grande do Sul, Minas Gerais and Paraíba to continue their election campaign. The following orientation was given to Paím Filho regarding various sections of the Liberal Alliance campaign program:

1. The decree of general amnesty for the 1922 and 1924 revolutionaries: Vargas informed the Senator that this was not an essential part of the program but that a special commission could be set up to study the situation.
2. Promise of electoral reform: The Senator was told that this also was not an inflexible part of the program.
3. Repeal of laws controlling the press: This point was not fundamental, and should Júlio Prestes object, Paím Filho could accept a compromise.

Vargas finally stated: "We are seeking a solution that bolsters the authority of the President of the Republic and, at the same time, opens a door for us to leave [the presidential race] without humiliation."[34]

At the same time he was working closely with politicians seeking a way out of the presidential contest, Vargas was playing a double game, for he was also encouraging Osvaldo Aranha to push his presidential candidacy. Aranha had coordinated detailed plans of action with Deputy João Neves. Neves had been sent to Minas Gerais in October to sound out the situation in that state. He reported in a letter to Osvaldo Aranha on October 28 that Antônio Carlos was eager to continue the struggle for the presidency and could promise "at least a minimum of 400,000 votes on March 1." Financially, the state would be in good condition to carry on a campaign for the Liberal Alliance as a result of a loan of $25 million from the Schroeder Banking group. The state had received and used $8 million; the other $17 million would arrive only in January, 1930.[35] Thus on one side Vargas appeared to be using the events in Minas Gerais to reach an understanding with the federal government, while at the same time, working with another set of aides, he encouraged and continued the electoral campaign.

In November, notwithstanding the plans for political accord, the tension on the national scene had increased. Former President Epitácio Pessôa injected himself into the campaign by declaring in the *Jornal do Comércio* on November 17 that he considered the President's statement regarding the free choice of Júlio Prestes by seventeen states untrue. He stated, "I cannot, unhappily, accept the explanation, which does not correspond to the facts. The President should not take the road of subterfuge but should declare frankly that he is convinced the orientation he has given the government is in the best interests of the Republic and should be continued."

Early in December Senator Paím Filho went to Rio de Janeiro to sound out Washington Luís on the possibility of a compromise candidate. Failing in this move, Senator Paím Filho then signed an astounding political pact which was later approved by Vargas: Vargas promised not to leave the state of Rio Grande do Sul to campaign for the presidency and if beaten in the election, would accept the result of the polls and support the incoming administration. In return, President Washington Luís and candidate Júlio Prestes gave a variety of pledges. Among them was the promise not to take any measures against citizens who supported the Vargas ticket. Federal office-holders connected with Vargas' Rio Grande do Sul Republican party were not to be dismissed or transferred. The pact further stated that winning candidates for the federal Congress who were members of the Vargas faction would not be challenged by Administration forces. It was also agreed that once the elections were over the relations between the federal government and the state of Rio Grande do Sul would return to their earlier harmony and friendship. Getúlio Vargas, if he won the election, promised to act in a similar manner toward the state of São Paulo.[36] This pact was known only to President Washington Luís, Júlio Prestes, Getúlio Vargas and the Senator.

Rumors began to circulate among other Rio Grande do Sul politicians that some accord had been made. Osvaldo Aranha, who was aware of the trip but did not know about the pact, communicated with João Neves, telling him not to vacillate or believe any of the rumors.[37]

As the election date approached, the world economic crisis destroyed the Washington Luís financial program, as well as the economy of the country, which was based upon the production and export of coffee. Liberal Alliance politicians used the economic situation to challenge the Administration in congressional debates. Feeling became intense. After December 18 the government majority remained away from the congressional sessions, leaving insufficient numbers for a quorum. Then Liberal Alliance politicians began to hold meetings on the steps of the national Congress building, to the great delight of the Rio de Janeiro populace. This situation lasted approximately one week.

On December 27 a federal deputy, Sousa Filho, was shot to death in the Congress.[38] Although the assassination was concerned in part with a personal feud, the Liberal Alliance politicians used it to agitate against the Washington Luís government. Political tension increased all over the nation.

On December 30, after a great deal of pressure from Borges de Medeiros, Osvaldo Aranha and members of the Liberal Alliance in Minas Gerais, Vargas broke one of the agreements in the pact with Washington Luís and Júlio Prestes: He went to Rio de Janeiro to read the program of the Liberal Alliance. The Washington Luís government refused to allow the Liberal Alliance party the use of any of the buildings in the city. Vargas became much more popular as a result, and delivered his speech in a public park, the Esplanada do Castelo, where more than a hundred thousand Cariocas heard him. Vargas' January 1, 1930, speech consisted of a reading of the Liberal Alliance program as it had been originally outlined in September of 1929. Among the many promises were: 1. amnesty for the revolutionaries of 1922, 1924, and 1926, 2. reorganization of the justice and education departments, 3. aid for the northeastern drought-stricken states, 4. aid to the agricultural sections of the country, 5. aid to the coffee planters, 6. development of the cattle industry, 7. acquisition of modern military equipment, 8. establishment of a better system of promotions in the army.[39]

After his enthusiastic reception by the people, Vargas remained only two days in Rio de Janeiro. He then went to São Paulo, where the Democratic party,[40] temporarily aligned with the Liberal Alliance in opposition to the São Paulo Republican party, had threatened to denounce Vargas if he did not make a campaign speech in the city. Vargas received an enthusiastic ovation in São Paulo, where he again read the Liberal Alliance program. On January 5 Vargas returned to Rio Grande do Sul. His campaign was over.

Meantime, the government candidate, Júlio Prestes, was making campaign speeches in various parts of the country. His program was similar to the Liberal Alliance program. Prestes favored continuing the monetary reforms of Washington Luís, lowering taxes, raising the income of the government officials, securing better army equipment and protecting industry.

On January 23 speakers from the Liberal Alliance went into the northeastern states and campaigned where Administration policy forces were firmly in control. When Liberal Alliance campaigners attempted to speak in Bahia, Pernambuco and Espírito Santo, a number of bloody encounters ensued. Many local politicians were using this opportunity to express long-standing political grievances. In February the Vice-President of Brazil, Fernando de Melo Viana, who had refused to support the Liberal Alliance although he was a native of Minas Gerais, was the victim of an armed attack in the city of Montes Claros, Minas Gerais. Two members of his party were killed and the Vice-President was wounded slightly. President Washington Luís used the attack to justify an order for more federal troops to enter the state. The capital, Belo Horizonte, was the scene of heavy federal troop concentration despite protests of Governor Antônio Carlos.

On February 27, 1930, two days before the election, Antônio Carlos was interviewed by a newspaper reporter to ascertain the attitude of the Liberal Alliance in the event it was defeated at the polls. He declared that the Liberal Alliance did not expect defeat, but if it did lose through fraud, this would constitute a revolutionary act by the Administration. In Rio Grande do Sul, Vargas on the eve of election simply restated the Liberal Alliance platform.

The elections, held on March 1, 1930, were orderly and carefully supervised. The returns did not correspond with the hopes of the ardent Liberal Alliance politicians. More than 1,000,000 votes were cast for Júlio Prestes and nearly 750,000 for Vargas.[41] In Minas Gerais, where Antônio Carlos had promised Getúlio Vargas more than 400,000 votes, only 307,000 were recorded for the Liberal Alliance,[42] although the candidate supported by Antônio Carlos for governor of Minas Gerais was elected with a clear majority.

Rio Grande do Sul cast more than 287,000 votes for Vargas and 789 for Prestes.[43] Paraíba declared 31,000 votes for Vargas and 10,000 for Prestes.[44] Vargas temporarily stepped down from the governorship to assure an impartial election, and turned over the state government to Osvaldo Aranha, who telegraphed a violent protest message to President Washington Luís. He implied that the election had been stolen from the Liberal Alliance because the federal government had "closed the voting places, adulterated results, frightened voters, bought votes, falsified voting lists and seized electoral rolls." [45]

Despite this telegram, all the elected federal senators and deputies of Rio Grande do Sul were accepted by the Administration. The other Liberal Alliance states of Minas Gerais and Paraíba did not have any political agreement with the federal government and were treated roughly. In Paraíba a federal investigating board loyal to Washington Luís checked voting irregularities. It decided that because of frauds, all federal representatives who had received Liberal Alliance support were disqualified. No one senator or deputy was acceptable to the Washington Luís Administration. In Minas Gerais the federal investigating board disqualified fourteen of the thirty-seven representatives of the Minas Gerais Republican party who had supported the Liberal Alliance campaign.[46] By this action the political power of Minas Gerais in Congress was effectively weakened.

The nation generally took the results calmly. The majority of the conservative politicians were prepared to accept the election of Júlio Prestes, but in Rio Grande do Sul the outcome divided the state into two groups. One was headed by Osvaldo Aranha, who favored a positive show of military force and revolution to change the election results. The other group, represented by Borges de Medeiros and Senator Paím Filho, favored a peaceful accommodation. Neither group was certain of Vargas' position. Borges de Medeiros had informed Vargas he could choose between two attitudes: "Send a telegram to Júlio Prestes congratulating him on his victory in the American manner, or direct a manifesto to the nation accepting the judgment of the ballot boxes." Vargas chose the second.

On March 19 Borges de Medeiros gave an interview that almost destroyed the Liberal Alliance party and nearly stopped the younger politicians favoring revolution. With regard to the election Borges de Medeiros declared: "In accordance with the last data, we find that Dr. Júlio Prestes has over 1,000,000 votes and Dr. Getúlio Vargas a little less than 700,000. We must therefore recognize frankly and loyally that Dr. Júlio Prestes is elected. There may be and there are many votes to be subtracted from these totals in view of frauds, which the electoral examining boards will find. These deductions will be proportional, as there were frauds in every state in the union, including our own. The electoral law, unfortunately, cannot prevent these things, and in view of our faulty civic education, there is no way totally to prevent such shameful practices.[47]

When questioned regarding the possibility of a revolution, Borges de Medeiros was equally emphatic: "Why have a revolution? Because we lost an election? But then it will be necessary for those who lose an election to revolt every four years, and the country would then be in a state of constant civil war. The job for all Brazilians is to unite to resolve the problems that face the country, and revolution will not solve these problems."[48]

Referring to revolutionary elements within the Republican party in Rio Grande do Sul, Borges de Medeiros declared that they were young, ardent and impassioned, but that they were also intelligent and disciplined and would submit to the will of the majority.

The interview of Borges de Medeiros was given nation-wide publicity and created a scandal among the more ardent members of the Liberal Alliance in both Minas Gerais and Rio Grande do Sul. Osvaldo Aranha, leader of the revolutionary element in Rio Grande do Sul, condemned Borges de Medeiros for his statements, and used this opportunity in an attempt to break the power of Borges de Medeiros. The opposition to the interview was so intense that Borges de Medeiros later claimed he had been misquoted. He declared also that the views expressed were his own and did not represent those of the Liberal Alliance party. Borges de Medeiros explained in a second interview the role of the Rio Grande do Sul Republican party. "Our orientation," he declared, "will be the traditional Republican one. Not unconditional support nor systematic opposition."[49] To these words Vargas gave his support.

Cutting across the pre-election scene and involved in the political developments was the figure of Captain Luís Carlos Prestes,[50] the

1924 revolutionary hero. Though he favored drastic economic reforms, he was condemned by the Communist party of Brazil, which was uncertain of his political orientation.[51] In 1930 the importance of Luís Carlos Prestes and his lieutenants was primarily in the military phase of the post-election period. Politically, Luís Carlos Prestes was important only insofar as the Liberal Alliance political leaders could link the name of this revolutionary with their cause. This was accomplished by the plank of the Liberal Alliance program that called for amnesty for the revolutionaries of 1922 and 1924.

In May, 1930, Prestes officially entered the Brazilian Communist party and directed this manifesto to the Brazilians: "The Brazilian revolution cannot be carried out with the anodyne program of the Liberal Alliance. A simple change of men, the secret vote, promises of electoral liberty, administrative honesty, respect for the Constitution, stable money and other panaceas, by no means interest the majority of the population, without whose aid any revolution that might be made would have the character of a simple fight between dominant oligarchies. Our blows must be directed against the two strongest points that support economically the present oligarchies—against the great landed property and against Anglo-American imperialism. These are the two fundamental causes of political oppression in which we live and of the successive crises from which we suffer. We live under the direct yoke of the bankers of London and New York City." [52]

When this statement was made public, the Liberal Alliance repudiated Prestes. Nevertheless, Liberal Alliance military elements continued to cooperate with his lieutenants. Previous attempts to form a political agreement between Luís Carlos Prestes and the Liberal Alliance had caused embarrassment to the conservative anti-Administration politicians. Many of the Liberal Alliance feared the radical element would control the organization. Governor João Pessôa of Paraíba constantly charged that the radical elements in the Liberal Alliance were too powerful.[53] Shortly before the election he was reported to have declared, "I will never support an armed movement. I prefer ten of Júlio Prestes to one revolution."

In the last week of March, 1930, the Minas Gerais governor, Antônio Carlos, attempted to destroy the influence of the Borges de Medeiros interview. Meeting with Gaúcho politicians who favored rebellion, the governor charged that Rio Grande do Sul was not complying with its part of the political pact signed with Minas Gerais in June, 1929. Antônio Carlos apparently believed that revolutionary action was the only way he could salvage control of the Minas Gerais Republican party. After the cooperation of former Presidents Epitácio Pessôa and Artur da Silva Bernardes was obtained for the military movement, a delegation of Minas Gerais politicians went to Rio Grande do Sul to arrange terms with Borges de Medeiros and Getúlio Vargas. On March 26, Vargas was approached, but he refused to take a definite stand with regard to the revolution. Despite Vargas' reaction, precise military plans for a revolution were formulated as early as April 11 by Osvaldo Aranha.

On the political level the battle was carried to the national Congress. A memorandum, written by the radical members of the Rio Grande do Sul Republican party and approved by Borges de Medeiros, declared that though the state would maintain official relations with the federal government, it would maintain an attitude of opposition to everything proposed by the federal government. Regardless of the action of the Rio Grande do Sul Republican party, Governor Vargas continued to maintain amicable relations with President Washington Luís. When the banks in the state of Rio Grande do Sul began to fail because of financial difficulties in April, 1930, Vargas requested a loan from the federal government. President Washington Luís complied immediately.

In the month of May the attitude of the Washington Luís Administration regarding the state of Paraíba became hardened. Few representatives were allowed in Congress who had cooperated with the Liberal Alliance. Governor Antônio Carlos of Minas Gerais protested to President Washington Luís. Vargas also issued a statement regarding the refusal of the federal government to seat the Paraíba representatives. He declared, "Today there is no divergence of opinion regarding the establishment of a spirit of tranquility. It depends upon a political policy of tolerance. There is great public pressure against the recent political events in Paraíba, and we cannot be far from the necessary rectification of these wrongs." [54] Members of the federal government in Rio de Janeiro interpreted this statement as a peaceful message, whereas the revolutionary elements in Minas Gerais and Rio Grande do Sul considered it decisive support for the revolution.

In June military preparations collapsed. Governor Antônio Carlos was convinced that Borges de Medeiros and Getúlio Vargas did not favor military action.[55] Antônio Carlos therefore requested the collaboration of Rio Grande do Sul in political action to prevent the federal government from destroying the Liberal Alliance in Paraíba and Minas Gerais. Though Osvaldo Aranha replied that political action was impossible, the Rio Grande do Sul military leaders failed to gain Vargas' positive support for a revolution. This resulted in the disaffection of the Minas Gerais Republican party. In Rio Grande do Sul, Osvaldo Aranha, apparently furious at Vargas, resigned at the end of June and sent a telegram to Minas Gerais politicians declaring he was finished "with the comedy. Impossible to continue under the direction of a chief so weak that he dampens the spirits of his own soldiers." [56]

Just as the danger of revolution seemed to be over, the assassination of Governor João Pessôa of Paraíba on July 26 changed the scene completely.[57] The revolutionary element assumed control. Although the assassination of the vice-presidential candidate had taken place as a result of a personal battle, the Liberal Alliance militarists once again had a cause. The killing of João Pessôa resulted from his order to have the police search the house of his political rival for arms and munitions. In their search the police discovered love letters, which were confiscated and promptly published in the official government newspaper of Paraíba.[58] The enraged politician shot João Pessôa. Liberal Alliance politicians who favored revolution were not interested in the reasons for the assassination. In the national Congress a Rio Grande do Sul deputy declared, "Cain, what have you done to your brother? President of the Republic, what have you done to the Governor of Paraíba?" [59]

Antônio Carlos sent a telegram to Vargas asking him for a joint protest to President Washington Luís, but Vargas refused. The revolutionaries interpreted his refusal as an indication that Vargas was ready to take more energetic action. Vargas' silence was interpreted by the Washington Luís Administration as an indication that he would do nothing. Vargas was an enigma. When federal troops were ordered to the state of Paraíba to suppress the anarchy that had developed in the capital as a result of rioting, Vargas simply declared, "I have the utmost confidence that these forces will remain faithful and loyal to the traditions of the national army respecting the autonomy of the state." [60] Liberal Alliance politicians had made the charge that Pessôa was murdered by the Administration and that the entrance of federal troops was a criminal act that jeopardized the autonomy of Paraíba.

The political situation was completely in the hands of the revolutionaries. In Rio Grande do Sul, Osvaldo Aranha now moved quickly and took advantage of the situation to force Borges de Medeiros to collaborate with the revolutionaries. Until the assassination of João Pessôa, Rio Grande do Sul had vacillated between the extremists and the conservatives, but in August Osvaldo Aranha convinced Borges de Medeiros of the necessity of revolution. The adherence of Borges de Medeiros meant that the state military brigades would now follow the revolutionary politicians.

A tighter plan of national action was coordinated. Political lines were clearly marked and roles assigned to individuals. In the north, former 1924 rebel Captain Juarez Távora and José Américo de Almeida were to play the most important roles. In Rio Grande do Sul, in the south, Flôres da Cunha, Lindolfo Color and João Neves would lead. Paraná would be handled by João Batista Luzardo and Plínio Tourinho. In Minas Gerais the help of Francisco Campos could be counted on. São Paulo would be handled by Moraes de Barros, and the Federal District by Mauricio Lacerda.

Aranha wrote to Raul Píla, an important political opponent in Rio Grande do Sul, on August 28, 1930, that Píla must have confidence in what Aranha was doing. The revolution was already on the march and nothing could stop it. Aranha stated that his role was that of a non-partisan coordinator of the revolution.[61]

During the month of September the governor-elect of the state of Minas Gerais, Olegário Maciel, indicated to Getúlio Vargas that he would cooperate with the military plans of the revolution. At the same time the new governor informed the President that he would fulfill his obligations to his state and to the country. This subtle message to the President resulted in the removal of most of the federal troops from Minas Gerais. Throughout September, despite repeated headlines such as appeared on September 3, 1930, on page 1 of the *Diário Nacional* of São Paulo that rumors of an armed revolt in Rio Grande do Sul were growing, President

Washington Luís continued to refuse to concede this possibility. He was sure the revolution could not take place because of the disagreements between the various Liberal Alliance political leaders. In addition, there had never been a successful military revolt in the history of republican Brazil. Theoretically, Washington Luís had the support of the army general staff, whose professional interests dictated that they remain loyal to the Ministry of War. The possibility of a small rebellion was even to be welcomed, since a successful show of force by the federal government would make the incoming Júlio Prestes government more secure. It would also divert attention from the distressing economic situation.[62] The absolute faith of Washington Luís in the army precluded any general preparations for defense against revolution. On October 3 the President telegraphed the governor of the state of Maranhão: "Despite rumors, the capital is peaceful."

The military revolution began at five o'clock on the afternoon of October 3. From this period on, the military element dominated the scene. Getúlio Vargas issued a proclamation:

> We are fighting a counterrevolution to reacquire liberty, to restore a pure Republican regime and for national reconstruction. We are a great movement of people fraternizing with soldiers from the valorous north to the extreme south. Rio Grande stands for Brazil; we will not fail in our heroic destiny.[63]

The Church appeared for the first time in the revolutionary movement when the Archbishop of Pôrto Alegre, Dom João Becker, issued a manifesto on October 3. He declared, "The revolution in Rio Grande do Sul is of purely political character and is not communistic. The social and religious institutions have not suffered. The national revolution will triumph inevitably." [64]

On October 4, Congress, obeying a request of Washington Luís, declared by a vote of 111 to 5 a state of siege in the Federal District and the states of Rio de Janeiro, Rio Grande do Sul, Minas Gerais, and Paraíba.[65] Throughout the three weeks, October 3 to 24, political action was subordinate to troop action.

Chapter 4

The Military and the 1930 Revolution

The role of the military in Brazil on both the state and federal levels had to be clearly defined before any successful extra-legal change of government could take place. The success of any positive political rebellion depended upon the willingness and ability of the protesting party to field a military force. This military unit had to be equal to the São Paulo state militia and federal troops, which remained temporarily loyal to the government. Brazil, up to 1930, had no tradition of successful military revolts. With the exception of the two small uprisings in 1922 and 1924, the republic had never faced a serious revolution.

Although the October, 1930, revolution may have been carried out to change the election results of March, 1930, there is sufficient evidence indicating that military operations were being planned well before the presidential election took place. As early as September, 1929, Luís Carlos Prestes was reported to have been approached by Osvaldo Aranha and offered the leadership of the rebel military forces. A group of Gaúcho political leaders went to Buenos Aires, where Prestes was living in exile, in an effort to win him over to the Liberal Alliance. Prestes refused to commit himself, although he accepted funds from Aranha to buy munitions for the future revolt. The majority of the lieutenants, however, gave their unqualified support to the revolution.

In the month of October, 1929, Aranha got in touch with federal army Lieutenant Colonel Pedro Aurélio Góes Monteiro, a native of northeastern Brazil, about the possibility of leading a military revolt after Colonel Euclides Figueiredo and Colonel Estevão Leitão de Carvalho had both refused to participate in any rebellion. A meeting was quickly arranged in Pôrto Alegre later in October, at which Osvaldo Aranha, Góes Monteiro, Congressman João Neves and 1924 rebel Lieutenant João Alberto met and formulated revolutionary plans.[1]

The Aranha files have also revealed a letter dated October 29, 1929, to Canadian Industries, Ltd., for the purchase of $241,750 worth of arms and munitions. Other correspondence indicates that various state military garrisons in Rio Grande do Sul had been sounded out concerning their possible support for a military uprising.

But no military action was taken before the election, and shortly after Júlio Prestes was declared the winner, General Gil de Almeida, federal commander of the Rio Grande do Sul military zone, wryly stated: "The elections that were held March, 1930, produced an exceptional resurrection of the dead, who turned up to vote for the candidates of the Liberal Alliance."[2] By March 8, 1930, Almeida had obtained detailed information concerning the arrival in Pôrto Alegre of some of the 1924 fugitive army officers. This information, together with previous advice, led him to believe that these rebels had returned to Brazil to aid in planning a revolution. He reported to Rio Grande do Sul state officials that the disappearance of federal rifles and munitions had increased.

Despite knowledge of anti-Federalist activity, it seemed that Getúlio Vargas and Borges de Medeiros were prepared to accept the election results. In the famous March 19, 1930 interview, Borges de Medeiros declared he was convinced "as never before that the people of Rio Grande do Sul will not take any steps to disturb the order of the country. I can make this statement not only in my name as head of the major political party, but also in the name of the governor, Getúlio Vargas, and all the secretaries of the state. I affirm that Rio Grande do Sul will keep order and peace, faithful to its traditions of respect to the constituted powers. I absolutely do not see that it would remedy existing evils, if they do exist, to apply an even greater evil, such as revolution."[3]

The views of Borges de Medeiros were not, however, shared by the more ardent and militant members of the Liberal Alliance. On April 11, Osvaldo Aranha met with anti-government political leaders from the states of Minas Gerais, Rio Grande do Sul and Paraíba to accelerate plans for a military revolution. A tentative military organization was set up. The revolution was to break out simultaneously in the three states. Osvaldo Aranha agreed to coordinate the movement in the south of Brazil and renewed his contacts with the 1924 rebel army officers. Colonel Nelson Etchegoyen was the liaison man between Aranha and the rebel lieutenants. João Alberto was made subchief of the general staff by Góes Monteiro, and Newton Estilac Leal became João Alberto's assistant. Both João Alberto and Estilac Leal were commissioned as colonels by Góes Monteiro when the revolution began. Góes Monteiro refused to accept a Vargas decree which commissioned him a division general, and assumed the rank of general only after the revolution succeeded.

In northeastern Brazil the plans were to be carried out by Governor João Pessôa of Paraíba, who had been the vice-presidential candidate of the Liberal Alliance. Juarez Távora, another 1924 rebel, was to command the military organization in the northeast. In São Paulo efforts would be made to win over a machine gun squadron to the revolution. In Minas Gerais, the state government would participate under the direction of Governor Antônio Carlos.

In Rio de Janeiro, Batista Luzardo, military coordinator for the nation's capital, cabled Aranha on April 2 to send to Rio de Janeiro one hundred thousand rounds of Mauser bullets, four machine guns and two instructors. Luzardo said he would pay for these expenses personally.[4] On April 12, Aranha placed an order for more than $800,000 worth of arms and equipment with a Czechoslovakian munitions factory.[5]

As a result of the campaign promises of the Liberal Alliance, organization of the rebel military forces was made easier. The federal military had been offered a program of army expansion, new equipment and a better system of promotions. These promises induced many officers to become partisans of the revolution.

In the month of May, Aranha decided that the revolution would begin July 16, 1930. Contact had been made with all the army officers in exile. Details for military preparations in the state of

Minas Gerais had been perfected, and the cooperation of certain São Paulo federal military garrisons had been arranged. But there then ensued a series of events which nearly forced the revolutionists to discard their plans. Siqueira Campos, one of the exiled 1924 army lieutenants, died in an airplane crash. He was to have provided the contacts in the state of São Paulo. In June Governor Antônio Carlos of Minas Gerais lost confidence in the military preparations of the state of Rio Grande do Sul, and the July date for the revolution was given up.[6]

An exchange of letters during June between Aranha and Antônio Carlos merely had the result of furthering distrust between the two officials. Aranha wanted unconditional support from the state of Minas Gerais, but Antônio Carlos, a cautious politician, refused to permit his state to become involved in the revolution until he saw more positive evidence that the Gaúchos were arming for a military uprising. The cumulative effect of these events produced a crisis in the revolutionary plans. Aranha resigned his post as secretary of the interior of Rio Grande do Sul, and João Alberto left Brazil and returned to Buenos Aires. At the end of June most of the dissatisfied elements felt that the opportunity for a successful revolution had been lost.

The federal government apparently had been aware of plans for the rebellion. Early in July Vargas told General Gil de Almeida: "The revolution will not pass the range of words, and rumors. This is the natural temperament of the Gaúcho. After the change of government in Minas Gerais [a new governor had been elected and was to take office in November], everything will pass because our arrangements are with Dr. Antônio Carlos and we have no agreements with Dr. Olegário Maciel [the governor-elect]."[7]

After the assassination of João Pessôa on July 26 by a political opponent who allegedly had the support of the federal government, the revolutionaries had a rallying point. The situation changed dramatically. Aranha now declared: "At this instant there isn't a single man in all of Rio Grande do Sul who can doubt the nature of the future that await us. The hour is near when the people of Rio Grande will redeem themselves from the insults with which the central power has sought to subjugate us."[8]

The rebel military plans were reorganized. Lieutenant Colonel Góes Monteiro, serving in the Rio Grande do Sul military region under General Gil de Almeida, had secretly accepted the position of chief of staff for the rebels as early as April, 1930. He now reactivated his plans.[9] Meanwhile, João Alberto had returned from Argentina to work with the newly appointed rebel chief of staff. Additional support came from Minas Gerais, as the death of João Pessôa had moved António Carlos to abandon his cautious role.

Loyal federal troops prepared to defend themselves. Intense military and political agitation in August forced General Gil de Almeida to increase federal forces in the strategic railroad city of Passo Fundo. As added defense against a possible revolution, he reinforced the military garrison at Pôrto Alegre.

João Alberto and others of the rebel army staff believed that their military preparations would be ready by the end of August. Plans were made for simultaneous attacks all over the country, but a few days before the date set for the revolution, Aranha was once again forced to change plans. The principal reason the revolution did not take place in August was the decision by Vargas that someone must go to Rio de Janeiro to communicate with federal military officials known to be well disposed toward the Liberal Alliance program.[10] Vargas wanted these officials informed of the revolutionary plans, and if the rebellion succeeded before rebel troops reached Rio de Janeiro, these military officials were to take over the government temporarily until the military forces arrived. Lindolfo Color, a young Gaúcho politician, was given the assignment.

Simultaneously the revolutionists began a propaganda campaign against loyal federal troops stationed in the state of Rio Grande do Sul. The theme was that brothers should not fight brothers. It was very effective, for the majority of the federal troops were natives of Rio Grande do Sul.

While news from Rio de Janeiro was awaited, great quantities of military supplies were unloaded at Passo Fundo. Despite the concentration of rebel military supplies, it was feared that the federal commander of the garrison would not join the revolution. Successful occupation of Passo Fundo would enable rebel troops to cross quickly into the state of Santa Catarina and thus carry the revolution northward to Paraná and the crucial state of São Paulo. Vargas dispatched a letter to the federal commander in Passo Fundo and invited him to join the rebels, but no definite commitments were made by the commander. Early in September, word finally arrived from Rio de Janeiro that the high-ranking military officers would not be able to aid the revolution, but promised to take over the government and keep order until the rebel forces arrived in the national capital, should the revolution succeed.

General Gil de Almeida kept pleading with federal authorities in Rio de Janeiro to take action against the revolutionary preparations. On September 3, 1930, he cabled the Ministry of War: "Intolerable situation as state authorities are protecting military deserters and openly inviting all to join the rebellion. I ask permission to concentrate troops in various parts of the state." [11]

On September 15, Almeida wired in code to General Nestor Passos, Minister of War, that he was certain Getúlio Vargas was disloyally participating in the revolution. Almeida also said he had seen through Vargas' device of letting him reach only Vargas' personal secretary, João Simplício, who honestly knew nothing about the revolution.

On September 25 at a meeting at rebel headquarters in Pôrto Alegre, the revolution was definitely scheduled for October 3. The revolt would take place at five-thirty in the afternoon in Rio Grande do Sul, Paraíba and Minas Gerais. This hour had been picked because government offices closed at five, and military headquarters would be deserted. Under these conditions it would be a simple matter to capture the federal commander of Rio Grande do Sul, General Gil de Almeida. In Pôrto Alegre the barracks of the state guard were in front of the federal army headquarters. For months the civil guard had lined up there when changing guard. This had been planned to avoid arousing suspicion of the day of the revolution, when instead of changing guard they would simply march into the army headquarters and take over. The attack against Almeida's headquarters was to occur five minutes early, so that when the major attack commenced in other parts of the state, Almeida would be a prisoner and unable to coordinate any defense.

On September 28, six days before the revolution, Almeida received secret information that the revolution was imminent. He demanded an interview with Vargas but was informed by the latter's secretary: "The state is in peace—a revolution is no longer possible." [12] September 30 found Rio Grande do Sul forces ready for battle. Effective mobilization had been accomplished by the municipal authorities in coordination with the rebel military staff, and the occasion of border incidents was used as an excuse to increase the state troops' concentration there. Three days later, October 3, the revolution began.

The role of Minas Gerais had been determined at the Pôrto Alegre meeting of April 18, 1930. It had been arranged that the Minas Gerais government would join the revolution simultaneously with Rio Grande do Sul and Paraíba. In view of the weakness of the state military forces of Minas Gerais, their role would be to distract the federal troops when the revolt started. The Minas Gerais soldiers were also to close the frontiers and thus immobilize federal troops who would normally have gone to fight the Rio Grande do Sul forces. Aside from military aid, Minas Gerais was pledged to contribute more than $30,000 for the purchase of arms and munitions.

The manufacture of war materials for the revolution was started in various factories in Minas Gerais. The Belgo-Mineira steel mill began to make hand grenades and a factory in Belo Horizonte made 75-millimeter artillery. The biggest problem faced by the Minas Gerais rebels was that the majority of the federal forces in their state were not Mineiros and would probably remain loyal to the government. Nevertheless, by June 13 three rebel military battalions were secretly organized.

The military preparations in the northeast of Brazil were on a smaller scale. As early as March, 1930, both military and civilian elements had arrived to help organize the coming revolution.[13] On April 14 Juarez Távora, a native of the northeast, had arrived in Paraíba to help plan the revolt. Progress was uncertain, until the July 26 assassination of João Pessôa created chaotic conditions in the state. Federal troops were prepared to occupy the state completely in the event of riots and bloodshed resulting from the assassination. Shortly before the death of João Pessôa, some federal troops had been transferred to the state to fight a local uprising and had remained on an alert to prevent any rebellion from elements of the Liberal Alliance. Nevertheless, the rebel military organization was constantly expanded under Juarez Távora, and federal units were approached in different sections of the state. Many promised to join the rebels on the day of the revolution. Using the same tactics that were employed in Rio Grande do Sul, the rebels chose the federal military headquarters as the first target of attack on October 3.

In Rio de Janeiro it was evident throughout the preparatory period that a revolution was imminent. To all appearances Washington Luís was powerless to halt the military developments. On August 29 the federal government allowed newspapermen to file dispatches to foreign countries declaring that rumors of revolutionary unrest in the southern part of Brazil were untrue.[14] On September 6 the Washington Luís government issued a press release stating that there were no indications of disorder in any part of Brazil.[15] From the amount of newspaper publicity given to the coming revolution it seems impossible that the Washington Luís government was not aware of events. On September 12 a *New York Times* dispatch from Montevideo, Uruguay, declared: "Despite the official statements of the Brazilian Government that tranquility is general throughout the Republic, Brazilian newspapers arriving here and statements made by prominent Brazilians to correspondents of Uruguayan newspapers disclose that there is widespread opposition to the Federal government and active preparations for a rebellion to be led by the state of Rio Grande do Sul. The military preparations are being directed against the Federal government."

At first the Washington Luís government believed that the date set for the revolution would be September 7, Brazil's independence day. On that day Rio de Janeiro was the scene of a large military review in which more than fifteen thousand troops participated. As October 3 drew closer, it was apparent that the government, preoccupied with the economic crisis, could do nothing to stop the coming revolution.

At three o'clock in the morning of October 3, Osvaldo Aranha and Góes Monteiro went to the Rio Grande do Sul government palace, where Vargas was awaiting information. In the governor's office Aranha informed Vargas that the revolution was to start that afternoon at five-thirty.[16] As the day progressed, rumors and warnings began to spread through the city. General Gil de Almeida was informed by enemies of the Liberal Alliance at one o'clock that the revolution was about to begin. Another message arrived at federal headquarters declaring that Aranha had issued a revolutionary manifesto. Shortly after two o'clock in the afternoon more telephone calls came to Almeida's office warning him that the revolution would start that day.[17]

Almeida alerted the federal garrison of Pôrto Alegre. Later in the afternoon reports from all the major cities of Rio Grande do Sul carried information of irregularities. Almeida sent a lieutenant to inform Vargas of disturbances and Vargas said, "Tell the General measures will be taken." [18] Although federal officers generally left the military headquarters at four-thirty, Almeida ordered no one to leave that afternoon. Despite this advance preparation, shortly after five o'clock the attack on army headquarters began. Within twenty minutes the federal military headquarters was in the hands of the revolutionists. Almeida refused to surrender officially until Vargas wrote him a letter requesting his surrender. Vargas guaranteed that he would be treated with respect.

By eleven o'clock that night, most of the federal troops of Pôrto Alegre had gone over to the rebels. The one exception was the Seventh Battalion of federal troops, which held out until the next day. On October 4 Vargas issued a proclamation. It declared, in part, the reasons for the revolution—the fraudulent presidential elections of March and the interference of the federal government in Paraíba. These events had made the revolution essential. He concluded: "Supported by public opinion and by most of the Brazilians within and without the country, and with the cooperation of the greater part of the armed forces, the revolution, strong in the knowledge of its justice and the power of its arms, hopes that the country will regain its sovereign rights without any more opposition on the part of the reactionaries." [19]

The rebellion went smoothly in southern Brazil. Most of the cities in Rio Grande do Sul went over to the revolutionists without fighting, and by the evening of October 4 few cities remained in the hands of federal troops. On October 5 the majority of the federal troops in the neighboring state of Santa Catarina joined the rebel forces, and it was only the capital of the state, Florianópolis, located on an island off the coast that offered any resistance. Paraná, the state north of Santa Catarina, capitulated to the rebels on October 6, three days after the revolution started. The number of rebel troops in the field was estimated at from twenty to thirty thousand.[20]

By October 10 the majority of the Rio Grande do Sul troops had been moved across the states of Santa Catarina and Paraná and were beginning to take up positions along the Paraná–São Paulo border. From October 12 to 20 there was a military stalemate near the border town of Itararé.[21] A battle was supposedly fought with up-to-date methods, with trenches running along the whole front, barbed wire, machine gun nests and artillery.[22] The two sides gave conflicting reports, but when it appeared that the front had been stabilized, the government troops began to retreat.[23] Itararé was crucial because the city was situated on the central north-south railroad line of Brazil. If the rebel military forces captured it, the road to São Paulo would be open to them.

The United States consul general in the city of São Paulo reported by telegram to the United States Secretary of State on October 18: "Government column advancing from Ourinhos badly defeated several days ago. The government is now on the defensive. São Paulo–Paraná railway rolling stock withdrawn and all bridges destroyed by the government. Whole São Paulo–Rio Grande railroad cooperating with the revolutionists." [24]

One of the results of the stalemate in the battle at Itararé was a request by rebel military headquarters for the Minas Gerais rebel forces to continue their military offensive for another five days, although they had been asked for only ten days of military action. While fighting was suspended at Itararé because of bad weather conditions, events in the other parts of the country had been developing in favor of the rebels. Troop action in Minas Gerais followed the same pattern as that in Rio Grande do Sul. Rebels occupied the federal headquarters in Belo Horizonte, the capital of Minas Gerais, shortly before five o'clock and captured the commander of the federal troops. The state troops succeeded in getting control of most of the federal garrisons, but one federal unit, the Twelfth Infantry Division, failed to surrender and held out until October 8.[25] Although the state government had carefully planned the military phase of the revolt, the majority of the federal troops did not join the rebels until the revolution started.

Federal troops surrounding the state of Minas Gerais were at a disadvantage because their lines were spread too thin. Their job was to protect the Rio de Janeiro–Minas Gerais frontier and also the São Paulo–Minas Gerais border. Taking advantage of the federal troops' long line of communication, rebel soldiers from Minas Gerais invaded the states of Espírito Santo, Bahia and Goiás.

The governor of Espírito Santo, upon being informed that an invasion had taken place, boarded a ship for Europe. The state was left in the hands of a provisional government, which joined the rebels. The Minas Gerais attack upon Bahia was an attempt to join Liberal Alliance forces advancing south from Paraíba.

Northeastern operations were controlled by Juarez Távora. The federal government had standing orders for his arrest; nevertheless, he had been moving about freely in the northeast for over six months.[26] By October 5, following the strategy set up in other rebel sections, the federal headquarters in Paraíba had been successfully occupied. The rebels triumphed without difficulty and by October 7, Natal, capital of Rio Grande do Norte, and Recife, capital of Pernambuco, joined the rebel forces and provisional governments were set up. In Pernambuco the rebel activity consisted of attacks by civilian reservists who had been called to service. They had armed themselves without consulting the Liberal Alliance military leaders and had captured the federal garrison.[27]

In a *New York Times* report on October 13 from Pernambuco, Juarez Távora stated: "The revolution is not mutinous in character, but is supported by all classes, including rich farm-owners, manufacturers, the middle classes, and working men. All Brazil northeast of the São Francisco River is in our hands.

"We are pleased to inform all nations through the Associated Press of the constructive purpose of the revolution which hopes to restore morality of administration and to re-establish Brazilian credit abroad by not abusing loans and by the practice of severe internal economy.

"It is entirely false that the movement has any connection with Bolshevist politics. It is important to note that the red badges worn everywhere are the badges of the old distinctive Liberal Party, embodying an enormous conservative strength."

The United States government entered the military scene late in the campaign as a result of a State Department decision on October 22 to place an embargo on the sale of arms and munitions to rebel forces.[28] In view of the general information sent to the State Department by the various consular officials in Brazil, it is surprising that this action was taken. It was naturally interpreted as an unfriendly act by the rebels and was also attacked in the United States press. In response, Secretary of State Henry L. Stimson issued a press release justifying his action.[29]

Rio de Janeiro from the onset of the revolution had been a source of conflicting information, as a result of government censorship of the press. According to the government-controlled press, the federal troops were winning all the battles and the rebels were routed on all fronts. Washington Luís had declared a state of siege in the states of Rio Grande do Sul, Paraná, Minas Gerais and Rio de Janeiro, and had also issued an order calling up all civilian reservists to serve in the army. When the government tried to enforce this order and demanded that reservists, regardless of their social, economic or political connections, report for active service, there was violent protest in Rio de Janeiro. The Liberal Alliance gained adherents in the capital of the country by this action of Washington Luís. Although *Excelsior,* a Mexico City newspaper, carried stories that President Washington Luís had lost the support of the army as early as October 12, 1930, it was not until the last days of the revolution that rumors began to circulate through Rio de Janeiro that the government was about to be overthrown.

In southern Brazil, inclement weather between October 20 and 24 delayed a general rebel offensive along the Paraná–São Paulo border. But on October 24, Lieutenant Colonel Góes Monteiro ordered a general offensive in the Itararé area.[30] On the same day, word reached rebel headquarters that a revolution had broken out in Rio de Janeiro. The rebel general staff called off the Itararé attack and made efforts to reach the headquarters of a military junta that had been set up in Rio de Janeiro.

This is the turning point of the revolution. It demands closer analysis. Although the initial military victories depended upon the state military forces of Rio Grande do Sul, the ultimate result was contingent on two other factors. The first was the adherence of the federal military units in São Paulo, Minas Gerais and Rio de Janeiro. The second involved the determination of the São Paulo Força Pública (state military forces) to defend their borders. If either the state or the federal army had decided to continue the military campaign, the struggle would have been long and sanguinary and the superiority of federal arms and equipment would probably have resulted in a victory for the legal forces. When high-ranking officers in Rio de Janeiro joined the rebels, it indicated that the usefulness of the Washington Luís Administration was finished, and it is safe to assume that some understanding with the Vargas forces must have been reached. It is at this point that the mysterious battle of Itararé becomes an interesting and unanswered point of study. Why did a seemingly irresistible revolutionary army sweep up to the São Paulo border and then stop there until a *coup d'état* in Rio de Janeiro settled the entire question.

There are several possibilities. One is that the São Paulo state forces were actually strong enough to stop the advancing armies of Lieutenant Colonel Góes Monteiro until the situation was changed by instructions from Paulista leaders to cease resistance. Regional jealousies were sufficiently strong that Paulistas would have balked at letting a Gaúcho army cross their borders unopposed.

The second possibility was that the federal commander of the São Paulo area would not capitulate until he received word from his superiors in the nation's capital. Another possibility was that bad weather really may have caused the delay. However, Getúlio Vargas' ability to seek out and generally obtain political, nonviolent solutions to difficult problems would point towards the possibility that some *modus vivendi* had been worked out between the Paulista coffee magnates and the leaders of the revolutionary forces. Promises must have been made to the São Paulo political and economic establishment assuring them that they had nothing to fear from the revolution.

On October 24, the junta, composed of Generals João de Deus Mena Barreto, Firmino Antônio Borba, Pantaleão Teles Ferreira and José Fernandes Leite de Castro, had overthrown the federal government in the national capital. Without consulting the rebel forces, they had sent a proclamation to President Washington Luís demanding his capitulation. The generals said that they felt the best interests of the country lay in accepting the revolution and in preventing more bloodshed.[31] When the President refused to believe that his top-ranking officers had joined the revolution, the junta then asked Cardinal Sebastião Leme da Silveira Cintra to serve as an intermediary to convince Washington Luís that he had no alternative but to resign. The Cardinal went personally to the President's residence and finally persuaded him to leave. Washington Luís was taken to Fort Copacabana for his protection, and he left the country a few days later.[32]

The military junta on October 24 had appointed General José Fernandes Leite de Castro as Minister of War and Colonel Bertoldo Klinger as chief of police of the Federal District. The appointment of General Hastimfilo de Moura to the position of military governor of São Paulo brought a storm of protests, since Moura had been in command of federal forces opposing the rebels in the São Paulo–Paraná area.

Rebel headquarters was surprised, for the junta's decisions had all been made without previous communication with them. Messages of protest began to pour into Rio de Janeiro from members of the Liberal Alliance party in São Paulo. Clarification was demanded by Vargas and Góes Monteiro. Telegrams were dispatched to the military junta in Rio de Janeiro. Vargas telegraphed on October 24:

> I am on the São Paulo border with thirty thousand men perfectly armed and acting in combination with the states of Rio Grande do Sul, Paraná, Santa Catarina, Minas Gerais and the north, not to depose Washington Luís, but to realize the program of the revolution. . . . I am merely a transitory expression of the collective will. Members of the junta of Rio de Janeiro will be accepted as collaborators but not as directors, since these elements joined the revolution at the time when its success was assured. Under these conditions, I will enter with the southern forces into the state of São Paulo, which will be occupied by troops I can trust. We will arrange the trip to Rio later. It is unnecessary for me to say that the march upon São Paulo and the subsequent military occupation is merely to guarantee military order. We have no desire to antagonize or humiliate our brothers from this state, who deserve only our esteem and appreciation. Before beginning our march for São Paulo tomorrow I want to hear any proposals that the junta may wish to make.[33]

Lieutenant Colonel Góes Monteiro, representing the military element of the Liberal Alliance, demanded:

> 1. The provisional government must have as its chief Dr. Getúlio Vargas, president of the state of Rio Grande do Sul, whom the revolution considers as the President-elect of Brazil, refusing to recognize frauds practiced by the executive and the legislative branches of the national government.

2. The position is justified not only by the fact that Dr. Vargas was elected by the popular will but also by his rank as commander-in-chief of the revolutionary forces directed against the regime which has just been overthrown. This opinion is definitely established among the leaders of the three states which led the revolt, Minas Gerais, Paraíba and Rio Grande do Sul, in agreement with the military and political elements of the entire nation.

3. A government headed by Getúlio Vargas will govern the nation without any previously assumed obligations except those principles set forth in the program of the Liberal Alliance, which headed the revolution.[34]

It was not until three days later, October 27, that the junta in Rio de Janeiro answered the telegrams of Vargas and Góes Monteiro. That day the junta declared, in a circular to the people, that they had finally made contact with the rebel forces and were awaiting the arrival of Getúlio Vargas before taking any further steps in organizing the government. On October 27, Osvaldo Aranha arrived in Rio de Janeiro. Getúlio Vargas would not enter the capital until it had been occupied by Rio Grande do Sul troops. Between October 27 and October 31, nearly three thousand Gaúcho troops arrived in the capital. On the night of October 31, after these troops had made Rio de Janeiro secure, Vargas, wearing a simple soldier's uniform, entered the city, and the junta of military officials turned the government over to him. An enthusiastic crowd of Cariocas cheered the arrival of the new head of the Brazilian nation. Almost unnoticed was the manifesto of Brazil's tiny Communist party, charging that the revolution was simply a fascist–military *coup d'état,* and the workers would suffer.

Chapter 5

The Collapse of the Coffee Economy

The critical condition of Brazil's economy in 1930 created an atmosphere favorable for the revolution. As federal and state government revenues dropped drastically an air of suspicion, uncertainty and recrimination developed. Everyone sought a scapegoat. Coffee, the main financial prop of São Paulo and the national government, easily became the chief target for the anti-Administration politicians. "General Café" may not have been the most important "general" aiding the rebels but certainly the coffee crisis contributed to their final triumph.

Coffee exports provided more than seventy per cent of the country's revenues in the 1920's.[1] Santos number 4, the most important type exported, sold on the New York Coffee Exchange in the following manner:

Cents per Pound	Marketing Year
19.0	1919–20
10.4	1920–21
14.3	1921–22
14.8	1922–23
21.3	1923–24
24.5	1924–25
22.3	1925–26
18.7	1926–27
23.2	1927–28
22.1	1928–29
13.2	1929–30
8.7	1930–31[2]

Control of the coffee price in Brazil had been turned over in 1925 to the newly established São Paulo Institute for Permanent Defense of Coffee. Whenever prices began to sag the institute bought and warehoused coffee and made loans on growers' stocks held in the warehouses and on coffee on the plantations. Funds for these operations were obtained through foreign loans and a transportation tax on every bag of coffee moved from the interior. The test for the Coffee Institute came in 1927–28, when a bumper crop of 27 million bags was recorded and the world price began to fall. The institute went into the New York market, bought coffee, kept stocks in the interior of Brazil and prevented a further lowering of prices. The strategy worked and the world price held. The 1928–29 crop was a small one and the Coffee Institute's reputation was high in the nation. The situation, however, was potentially dangerous, for the high price of coffee artificially maintained by state government purchases tempted Brazilian planters to expand production. Columbian and Central American planters also increased their outputs. Each year it became more difficult for the government to buy the surplus of Brazilian coffee and to keep the world price up.

The price of coffee determined the rate of exchange and also provided the dollars to service foreign loans.[3] When Washington Luís was elected in 1926, Brazil's foreign indebtedness was approximately $900 million.[4] The annual interest on these loans and other foreign investments amounted to nearly $175 million, and Brazil counted on a favorable trade balance to provide gold to meet these payments. Coffee was the key to the situation. In May, 1929, an economic crisis developed when the price of coffee began to decline rapidly. The coffee surpluses of the previous year and the certainty of another heavy crop resulted in the possibility of the world market's being flooded with coffee. This situation created a weakness in the Brazilian monetary exchange. A decrease in the volume of foreign loans to Brazil and the tightening of credit in both the United States and Europe forced the national government to order the Bank of Brazil to limit credit severely.[5] This, in turn, resulted in the São Paulo banks cutting back and calling in their loans to coffee planters.

In June, 1929, rumors of a split in the Administration caused uneasiness in political circles regarding the 1930 presidential elections, and in August, 1929, it appeared that the Washington Luís Admininstration might be faced by a strong opposition candidate, Getúlio Vargas, running against Júlio Prestes, the choice of Washington Luís. Vargas, though opposing the Washington Luís government politically, stated in an interview August 11, 1929, that he favored both the financial program of the Administration and continued subsidies for coffee. These statements were repeated by Vargas on September 3, 1929.

Later in September, the director of the São Paulo Coffee Institute declared that the policy of coffee subsidies was sound and that no change would be made, because none was required. This speech was hailed in Brazil, and everyone assumed that the institute had the resources to buy the surplus of the next coffee crop. But when the New York stock market crash occurred three weeks later, the slowly declining price of coffee fell drastically.

On October 11, 1929, a vivid description by the British economist, J. W. F. Rowe, explained the situation on the Santos Coffee Exchange: "The broker who usually conducted the Coffee Institute buying in public operations sat quietly in his place and made no bid to buy. But, while very astonished, the market appears to have thought that he was engaged upon some new bluff, and no attempt was made to call it by offers to sell at reduced prices. At the afternoon session, however, he again remained silent, and the market suddenly realized that the end had come. The price fell the full limit allowed at any one session and this was repeated at succeeding sessions. New York and other markets of course followed suit. Though the headlong fall was soon checked, the price continued to decline sharply and almost continuously so that by December 1, 1929, New York was quoting 15 cents a pound compared with 22 cents before the crash." [6]

The effect upon the national economy was profound. The fall in the price of coffee not only quickly curtailed national income but also sharply reduced government revenue, with the result that the servicing of loans was made more difficult than ever. The exchange would have fallen further if the national government had not begun to export gold reserves to New York and London.

As a result of the break in the coffee price, the São Paulo government faced bankruptcy. State officials immediately appealed to the national government for either an issue of notes, which would enable the state to supply more credit to the coffee planters, or a moratorium. President Washington Luís refused to grant either of these requests. At this point the Administration may have lost the confidence of the São Paulo planters and thus opened a breach in the previously solid front of support they had demonstrated for Washington Luís. It is probable that the national government did not have the credit or the financial resources to support the demands of the São Paulo government. Part of the explanation of Washington Luís' action may be found in the following financial report of the Banque Française et Italienne of October 17, 1929: "The Coffee Defense is absorbing more and more resources and the Banco do Brasil is no longer equal to the occasion, despite the important funds granted to it. As a matter of fact, from the end of September and the beginning of October, the rumor has been widespread that this bank had stopped its advances against bills of lading. Due to this fact there has resulted a well understood feeling of uneasiness, increased by the alarming news concerning the drop in coffee prices in New York. Later it was announced that the bank of São Paulo had obtained—not without laborious negotiations—an advance of 100,000 contos [$5 million] from the Banco do Brasil to the end of being able to continue to function.

"It is here that we come face to face with the antagonism that exists—between the financial policy of the federal government aiming at the re-establishment of the equilibrium in all its affairs and the policy of the coffee defense based on the artificial limitation of offerings." [7]

At the close of 1929 the coffee stabilization program was demanding more and more of the financial resources of the national government, thus destroying the financial program of Washington Luís, which was based on sound currency. Long before he became President in 1921, he had opposed the use of the financial resources of the national government to buy up surplus coffee to keep the price high.[8] But by 1926 when this former São Paulo governor was elected, he stated that the country's prosperity depended upon the valorization [9] of coffee and a sound currency. However, in 1929 it appeared that the President was again convinced that the gearing of the national financial structure to coffee was an unhealthy economic situation and would doom any program of financial and economic reorganization. When the economic crisis developed in 1929, he was apparently determined that economic stabilization for the whole country on a broader base was more essential than the maintenance of the coffee economy of the state of São Paulo. The *Correio Paulistano,* official organ of the São Paulo Republican party, reported on October 19, 1929, that rumors that the federal government had abandoned coffee price support were false. Yet throughout the month the newspaper reflected the fears of the coffee planters. The idea has been advanced that the President favored the small but rapidly developing industrial and commercial interests of the country in opposition to the agrarian coffee-planter interests.

Meanwhile, the situation in the state of São Paulo became desperate. Failure to obtain federal aid forced the state to turn to foreign bankers. As early as November, 1929, a loan was reported to be under negotiation with London and New York bankers.[10] This was not an easy task, since the stock market crash in the United States signaled the beginning of a period of restricted financial activity. The Schroeder bank representative in Brazil informed Paím Filho and João Neves that the São Paulo state government was having a great deal of difficulty borrowing money, and although a loan had been granted to the state, it was necessary to form a group of eleven banks for this purpose.[11] By December, 1929, banks all over Brazil were forced to limit their credit more and more. Many stores reported a 40 per cent drop in business transactions by mid-December.[12]

Merchants and shopkeepers found business declining. Imports ceased, trade was stagnant and the manufacturing industries of São Paulo were nearly all idle. Planters began to shut down their city homes and return to the country. Nevertheless the majority of the coffee planters felt that the drop in the coffee price was merely a result of a temporary market break, which did not justify the Washington Luís Administration's refusal to grant an extension of credit or a moratorium to the Paulistas.[13] The opposition of the coffee planters to the national government probably crystallized in this period.

These developments were reflected on the national political scene in the increased tempo of the presidential campaign between Getúlio Vargas and Júlio Prestes. On January 1, 1930, Vargas came to Rio de Janeiro and in a campaign speech made a number of statements assuring the coffee planters of his support of the coffee valorization program. Vargas also re-emphasized his desire to continue the financial program of the Washington Luís Administration. There can be no doubt concerning Vargas' political astuteness, for these pronouncements satisfied many coffee planters and at the same time satisfied opponents of the coffee program. The economic chaos created by the coffee crisis was an important factor in setting the stage for the revolution. The coffee planters blamed the financial distress of the country on the incompetence of the President.

By February, 1930, the Brazilian government had shipped more than $22 million in gold bullion to the United States to meet the deficit in the balance of payments.[14] Coffee prices remained low, currency values fluctuated and foreign credit was reported to be held up awaiting the outcome of the March, 1930, presidential elections.

When Administration forces won out in the elections and Prestes gained a narrow victory over Vargas, the *Tea and Coffee Journal* stated: "It is hoped that last week's presidential election will prove a happy event without being followed by political disturbances, and that under the coming administration the many serious problems facing Brazil will find a favorable solution." Apparently the election satisfied the American banking interests, for in April, 1930, the long-negotiated loan to the state of São Paulo was finally made for $100 million.[15] Nearly half of the loan went to service old debts, so that the amount of new money that actually came to Brazil was only $55 million.[16] During the loan negotiations it was understood that the money would enable the São Paulo government to buy the surplus 1929–30 coffee crop and keep it off the world market, thus stabilizing the price. However, instead of a small crop of 8 million bags, as estimated by the São Paulo Coffee Institute, a record-breaking 29 million bags were harvested.[17] When news of this harvest reached the world trading centers, coffee prices, which had been stabilized at fourteen cents a pound, began to drop.

The deep interest of United States business firms in the economic condition of Brazil was highlighted in June, 1930, by the good will visit of President-elect Júlio Prestes. Though Prestes refused to discuss the economic situation in Brazil or the coffee problem, the *Tea and Coffee Journal* reported: "Having recently participated in a large loan intended for the stabilization of the São Paulo coffee situation, New York businessmen are observing all the steps to be taken in Brazil toward fulfillment of the purposes announced in the loan contract. As these purposes, in turn, have a bearing upon the coffee market during the forthcoming years, coffee roasters, brokers, and traders throughout this country have more than a casual interest in any Brazilian policies described or even hinted by the new president-elect." [18]

The economic situation continued to deteriorate in Brazil. At the end of July, as a result of the 29-million-bag crop, the coffee price fell to ten cents a pound. The economy was in danger of collapse as the surplus threatened to force prices even lower. The coffee planters were aware of the hostility of Washington Luís and of the precarious financial situation of the national government, which precluded any monetary aid for São Paulo. In a report for July, 1930, Moody's Investment Service stated that Brazil's foreign indebtedness had reached over $1,181 million, of which almost three-fourths was owed by the national government. The service of these foreign debts was reported to be approximately $200 million, which could be paid for only by increased coffee exports or further loans.[19]

After the assassination of João Pessôa in the last week of July, President Washington Luís may have realized the danger of both his political and economic situations, and he changed the previous position of unequivocal opposition to committing federal finances to support of the São Paulo coffee structure. The federal government in July again took over the responsibility of supporting the price of coffee.

Before the Brazilian Congress in August the President stated: "If stabilization is indispensable to coffee, coffee is indispensable for stabilization. To the causes of the slight monetary depreciation amongst us—a reflection of the worldwide financial crisis—we must add the insufficiency and rigidity of our banking institutions. The apprehensions caused by the threat of disorders in connection with the presidential campaign restricted our exports to neighboring countries and interrupted the stream of capital, mostly American, which was flowing into our country." [20]

The economic situation did not improve, and on September 3, 1930, the *New York Times* reported that the Brazilian government had shipped over $1 million in gold bullion to New York and London. This shipment, along with a number of others, reduced Brazilian gold reserves to about $70 million.[21] Normally, the gold reserve of Brazil was about $100 million. Approximately five days before the revolution began, an editor of the influential *Tea and Coffee Journal* commented: "Recent political disturbances in three states of Latin America, Bolivia, Peru and Argentine—in which the executive heads were deposed—have been productive of a number of rumors regarding possible like changes in others of our southern neighbors. Unsupported by facts these reports of instability have had the effect of causing uneasiness and hesitancy on the part of the foreign investors in utilities in those countries. Furthermore, such statements are reflected in the European and American bond markets where securities of Latin America are bought and sold.

"This matter of adverse rumors is ever a distressing one. Tricksters and speculators are always ready to take advantage of the inconveniences that they occasion.

"At times they even go beyond the rumor stage and become reality—through too much literal acceptance by the public. When hearing such reports, it is always well to remember that human nature and its behavior are much the same with others as with ourselves. National honor and credit are just as dear to one country as to another. Rumor or no rumor we believe that no Latin American state will sacrifice these under any conditions other than through physical catastrophe." [22]

During this period of economic instability more than a million persons directly connected with the coffee industry in the states of São Paulo, Minas Gerais and Rio de Janeiro were affected by the adverse conditions.[23] The majority of the Brazilian rural workers were landless laborers whose average wage was extremely low in contrast with that of urban workers. When the stock market crash lowered the value of Brazilian coffee in the world market, coffee planters were forced to cut labor costs to a minimum. Wages were not paid, and many coffee workers were living at subsistence level on food planted between the coffee trees. Their diet, generally poor and inadequate even in good times, became more meager. A feeling of unrest began to permeate the rural areas of the south.[24] Many workers began to migrate to the larger cities, and São Paulo newspapers reported the mushrooming of "shanty towns" in various sections of the city.

Mixed with the newly arrived rural workers were the unemployed urban laborers. Over six thousand persons a month used the food and shelter facilities provided by the city of São Paulo.[25] As these arrangements were inadequate, the *Diário Nacional,* one of the leading newspapers, suggested that the more than one thousand empty factory buildings be turned into temporary barracks for the unemployed.

Civil servants who had lost their jobs when the government's financial condition forced a drastic reduction in personnel also swelled the ranks of the discontented. The states of Paraná and São Paulo were at least four months behind on salary payments to their state employees.[26] Hundreds of thousands of persons were dependent upon the government for their livelihood. These people lived on extremely narrow economic margins, and after losing their jobs were unable to enter private enterprise because of economic limitations or for reasons of social prestige.[27]

Though an undercurrent of discontent existed, the mass of urban Brazilians were not locked in a struggle with the police or the military. The apathy of the unemployed in São Paulo was broken occasionally by the remark, "Isidoro is coming soon." This was a reference to Isidoro Lopes, a popular army officer who led an unsuccessful rebellion in 1924.

There were no dangerous or significant public disorders prior to October 3, 1930, and no special precautions were planned by either state or federal officials to maintain law and order. The depressed economic conditions had resulted in great hardship for many, but the situation had not reached the explosive stage. The revolution began before this could occur.

Foreign capital activity in Brazil provided another dimension to the economic milieu of the October, 1930, revolution. Competition between the United States and Great Britain for economic supremacy in Brazil through trade and capital investment intensified during the 1929 stock market crisis. It undoubtedly contributed to internal political antagonisms of the period. Pending further research, the direct importance of this competition to the revolution cannot be assessed. That the United States business community supported one political faction and Great Britain another also is a subject for investigation.

The Brazilian press commented openly on the bids for economic supremacy, noting the contest in public utilities between United States Electric Bond and Share Company and the Canadian-owned Brazilian Traction, Light and Power Company, Ltd., which controlled the communications and utilities system of Rio de Janeiro. In June, 1930, it was rumored that Brazilian Traction would be bought by Electric Bond and Share, but this transaction never materialized.[28] When Henry Ford was granted extensive concessions to set up a rubber plantation in the Amazon River area, the government allowed British businessmen similar privileges. Railroads in the Santos–São Paulo area were also fought over.[29] During the 1920's, Great Britain had gradually lost ground to the United States in both import and export trade with Brazil.[30] Shortly before the revolution the British had sent two commercial missions to Brazil in an attempt to integrate and improve trade conditions between the two countries. In addition to seeking new trade the British were vitally interested in their more than $1-billion investment in the country.[31] In 1930 United States capital investments amounted to little more than half that amount but rapidly expanded after this period.

The evidence seems to indicate a shift of financial control, and must be viewed against a background of world economics as a movement of international capital. A 1930 report of the British Commercial Office declared: "United States capital has shown a certain tendency to acquire control of companies of British ownership and under British management." [32] Even though British investments in 1930 were more than double those of the American financial interests, the greater part of the iron and manganese deposits of Brazil were controlled by the United States Steel Corporation.[33] In addition, Electric Bond and Share controlled most of the public utilities in five of the major states of Brazil, and the meat-packing firms of Armour and Company, Swift and Company and Wilson and Company had extensive holdings in the cattle industry of Rio Grande do Sul. In the north, cotton and cottonseed oil products were controlled by American-owned Anderson Clayton and Company.

On October 27, 1930, after the twenty-one day military phase of the revolution was past, Vargas was questioned concerning foreign investments, and he declared: "We will respect in their entirety all obligations assumed by Brazil prior to October 3." [34] This was Vargas' assurance that the revolution would not endanger the position of the foreign investor in Brazil.

In reviewing the economic events that directly contributed to the revolution, it is apparent that the unsound financial condition of Brazil can be traced to the narrow base upon which the country's foreign trade operated. Israel Pinheiro, an important Minas Gerais politician, commented on the economic aspect of the revolution: "Coffee valorization brought about by the Taubaté Convention was the initial cause of the 1929 crisis and the decisive factor that precipitated the 1930 revolution. The banner of the revolution may have been apolitical, but the causes were economic."[35] The sharp drop in the price of coffee, brought about by overproduction and the collapse of the world market, destroyed the financial structure of the country and temporarily weakened the influence and power of the state of São Paulo.

Getúlio Vargas took full advantage of the situation, but at no time did he attack the coffee planters. The platform of the Liberal Alliance was carefully phrased so as not to give offense to the Paulista coffee magnates. Vargas posed no political or economic threat to the coffee planters, whereas the Washington Luís administration had at one point refused financiad aid to São Paulo. Not only the Coffee Institute but Washington Luís, President-elect Júlio Prestes and the entire Administration had blundered in the eyes of the general public and created the conditions that had resulted in the country's chaotic financial predicament. The coffee barons were in the same position as the United States banking community when all the financial institutions closed in 1933. For a brief moment they were completely discredited.

To salvage the situation the Paulista coffee planters may have felt that a political scapegoat was needed, and the Washington Luís Administration and President-elect Júlio Prestes served this purpose perfectly. The economic situation in the post-election period was reaching a point where the policy of coffee control would have to be discarded. If this happened and coffee controls were abandoned completely, the flood of coffee would probably bankrupt every Brazilian bank, as well as the federal and state governments. Foreign trading firms would suffer severe losses and the leaders of Brazilian politics, industry and commerce would be ruined. The Vargas-led revolt was welcomed in São Paulo economic circles. Whether any additional promises were made by Getúlio Vargas during the three weeks the Gaúcho armies were stopped at the borders of São Paulo is unknown, but the coffee planters probably gave their tacit approval to the armed rebellion.

Chapter 6

Vargas and the Political Structure: 1930 to 1945

In the years between 1930 and 1945 Brazil was dominated by Getúlio Vargas. He was the government for fifteen years, and every major shift in national policy carried his imprint. During this period the country's traditional economic foundation was changed by the men from Rio Grande do Sul who surrounded Vargas and replaced the Paulista coffee planters as the rulers of the nation. The one-crop economy gave way to a broader based agricultural and industrial structure. Politically, the power shift is even more sharply etched. São Paulo and Minas Gerais after 1930 no longer exclusively determined the affairs of the nation. Gaúcho politicians swarmed into Rio de Janeiro and in the next decade and a half took over the administrative machinery of Brazil.

The period 1930 to 1945 breaks clearly into three units. October, 1930, to July, 1932, was a period of transition for the new regime. In July, 1932, a rebellion against Vargas broke out in the state of São Paulo but was crushed by September. From September, 1932, until November, 1937, was another distinct unit of Brazilian political history. A quasi-democratic state existed, which drafted and functioned under the 1934 Constitution. November 10, 1937, to October 29, 1945, was the third and final period of the Vargas reign. Certain trends and developments that were begun during these latter years still persist in the Brazilian contemporary political scene. On October 29, 1945, Getúlio Vargas was relieved of his office, and the military permitted Brazil to resume a republican and democratic form of government.

From October, 1930, to July, 1932, the aims of the revolutionaries were not clearly focused and as a result they had few definite plans or programs to present to the people. It was government by improvisation. Almost immediately a power struggle began between those elements within the revolutionary party who wished to bring about profound social reforms, and those who desired technical reforms that would attack and solve the problems of the day and leave the question of deep social changes for a later period. In this second group were Getúlio Vargas, Góes Monteiro and Osvaldo Aranha.

The more advanced and radical of the revolutionaries were in a weaker position, for they did not have a precise program and, more important, they did not have control of the new government machinery to carry out their rather vague ideas of social reform. Many lieutenants of the earlier 1922 and 1924 rebellions were in this group, but they were quickly squeezed out of power by the conservatives.

Thus the political reorganization that began in October, 1930, had few ideological guidelines. It was more a pragmatic response to national problems viewed from the perspective of politicians from the state of Rio Grande do Sul. Profound social and economic reforms were not foremost on the list of objectives of the leaders of the revolution. Many of these leaders may have felt there were injustices in the Brazilian political structure but that these were purely of a mechanistic nature. The most important items were improving the electoral machinery, establishing the secret ballot and reducing the economic and political power of the state of São Paulo in the federal political structure. But hard-core social and political reform programs were lacking. Some elements did feel that the bad economic conditions of the period indicated that sharp breaks with the past traditions of Brazil were needed in the area of social legislation. But the most powerful of the revolutionaries, Getúlio Vargas and Góes Monteiro, were cautious politicians.

The provisional government set up on November 3, 1930, clearly reflected the mixed reform-and-conservative character of the revolution. Getúlio Vargas, Góes Monteiro and Osvaldo Aranha put together the following cabinet: Foreign Affairs, Afrânio de Melo-Franco; Justice, Osvaldo Aranha; Treasury, José Maria Whitaker; War, General José Fernandes Leite de Castro; Navy, Admiral Isaías de Noronha; Transportation and Public Works, Captain Juarez Távora; Agriculture, Joaquim Francisco de Assis Brasil; Education, Francisco Campos; and Labor, Lindolfo Color.

Basically, the cabinet was a conservative one with reformers Color and Campos given the newly created ministries of Education and Labor. Juarez Távora was perhaps the most radical, but his area of operation was the northeast part of Brazil, which had only a secondary relationship to the heartland of the country. The War and Navy ministries were essentially puppets, since Góes Monteiro had become chief of staff and dominated the armed forces. Throughout the next fifteen years Vargas' control of the country depended to a large extent upon the support of Góes Monteiro and his command of the Brazilian military. It was difficult to separate the careers of the two men.

General Góes Monteiro insisted that the illusion of legitimacy and continuity within the regular army be maintained. Few high-ranking generals lost their posts, and no scars were opened up within the army as result of the revolution. Yet at the same time, Góes Monteiro was a realist. He took no chances with the army and maintained an informal Revolutionary Army Staff Headquarters which kept the Brazilian military establishment off balance. It was only on April 18, 1931, amid much public notice, that Góes Monteiro announced that the services of the Revolutionary Army Staff Headquarters were no longer needed and it was to be disbanded.

Both the Foreign Affairs and Treasury ministries were given to men who were intimately connected by previous experience and family ties with their assignments. The Agriculture post was given to Assis Brasil to assure local political unity in the state of Rio Grande do Sul. Osvaldo Aranha's appointment as Minister of Justice was a popular one, as his flamboyant speeches kindled the imagination of the people.

To get the wheels of government moving again, the executive office began to govern by issuing presidential decrees. These decrees were considered legal and binding and carried the President's signature as well as that of the appropriate cabinet minister.

Decree Law 19.398 of November 11, 1930, set up the administrative machinery for the new provisional dictatorial government. It was a relatively short document of eighteen articles, commencing with the simple statement that Getúlio Vargas was the chief executive with discretionary power delegated to him in every area of the new provisional government. The second article dissolved the Congress. Article 5 suspended all constitutional guarantees of the citizens. Article 11 changed most of the state governors and placed the various states under the control of administrators called Interventores. These men were to be selected by Getúlio Vargas and were to have both executive and legislative power.

Article 11 turned out to be quite troublesome, and created problems that plagued the new revolutionary government from 1930 to 1932. Many young military officials considered personally loyal to Getúlio Vargas and Góes Monteiro were sent to take over control of the various states. They were to organize political machines that could be integrated with the central Administration. The problem was that the central government had no concrete plans for the reorganization of the country, and Brazil had no tradition of strong national control in planning and programming.

Selection of the Interventor for São Paulo was a very important decision, and when former Lieutenant João Alberto Lins de Barros was appointed on November 24, 1930, the state was stunned. He was an unknown quantity to the Paulista elite. At this point it is apparent that the death, early in 1930, of Lieutenant Siqueira Campos, who was a Paulista and might have bridged the gap between the Gaúchos and the politicians of São Paulo, was a greater tragedy nationally than had been supposed. João Alberto, a northeasterner and a prominent member of the Luís Carlos Prestes column, was keenly aware of the injustices of the Brazilian economic system and felt, as did many, that the state of São Paulo was the direct cause of much of the poverty and misery existing in the northeast. Northeasterners argued that they were a depressed colony of the Paulistas, supplying them with cheap labor, raw materials and secure markets for their manufactured goods. João Alberto was, however, trusted by both Getúlio Vargas and General Góes Monteiro, insofar as Vargas and Góes trusted anyone.

The Vargas regime was aware that any successful national reform program had to be carried out first in São Paulo. All political or economic proposals by the new Interventor would naturally reflect the attitudes of the revolutionary government in Rio de Janeiro. Thus every move by João Alberto was closely scrutinized and analyzed by Paulista political leaders.

No major actions were taken in December, but on January 5, 1931, through state Decree Law 4814, the most vocal of the opposition newspapers was taken over by the revolutionaries. João Alberto was not going to permit any resistance to his administration. When the Interventor next encouraged the organization of a club that carried the interesting name Society of Friends of Russia, the São Paulo elite became clearly hostile.[1] João Alberto had further difficulty in building support in São Paulo when he decided to ignore the Democratic party, which had supported Getúlio Vargas in the election and the revolution. The party was split on the issue of allying itself with João Alberto and had little projection outside the capital. It soon became apparent that João Alberto was going to create a political apparatus that would be linked closely with the Gaúchos in Rio de Janeiro.[2]

In the economic sector, the coffee interests were jolted by Decree Law 4815 of January 6, 1931, which resulted in the reorganization of the Coffee Institute. It was now placed under the personal and direct control of the Interventor. This meant that all stockpiling and marketing activities of coffee, both internally and externally, were to be directed by the Vargas machine and not by the elite of the state of São Paulo. From this point on, a cold war began in the state. On January 7, 1931, Decree Law 4819 was issued, stating that a special bureau would be set up to assist needy rural workers. The João Alberto Administration had begun to build a following among the poor.

The resentment against the Vargas regime and João Alberto that continued to build up in São Paulo among the middle class and the elite was compounded of many factors. Foremost was the fact that São Paulo was not being governed by Paulistas and the reforms being made were not those desired by the former political leaders of the state. Finally, in July, 1931, João Albert resigned as Interventor, as the Vargas Administration made an effort to ease pressure in São Paulo by appointing Paulista political figureheads.

However, opposition continued to mount and, in addition to constant assertions that the São Paulo government was mismanaged, the Paulistas charged that Vargas was not honoring his pledge to give the Brazilians a new constitution. Paulistas began to conspire against the Vargas regime. As early as March, 1931, a plan for an armed rebellion was organized but collapsed when state military elements could not agree on a coordinated plan of action. Contact, however, was made with discontented politicians in the states of Rio Grande do Sul and Minas Gerais.

The Vargas regime reacted to the growing discontent by promulgating Decree Law 21.402 on May 14, 1932, calling for elections on May 3, 1933, of representatives to a constituent assembly that would prepare a new constitution for Brazil. The announcement came too late.

On July 9, 1932, an armed insurrection broke out in São Paulo against the government. The rebels expected support from Rio Grande do Sul and from the commanding general of the Mato Grosso area, but no aid was forthcoming from either area. General Bertoldo Klinger flew in from Mato Grosso but brought no troops with him.[3] João Neves and Borges de Medeiros broke with Vargas and tried to get Rio Grande do Sul to join the revolt, but failed when Interventor Flôres da Cunha switched his position at the last minute and remained loyal to Vargas. João Neves' statement to the nation rather accurately explained the political situation in Brazil at that time. The Vargas government, he charged, was one of "clubs and clans, of promises and fictions, of lies and imaginary salaries, secret groups and favored persons without a program."[4]

The federal government moved swiftly. General Góes Monteiro, who had briefly considered joining the Paulista rebels, remained loyal to Vargas and dispatched government troops to surround the state. Support for the federal government poured in from all the other sections of Brazil, which feared that São Paulo was attempting to re-establish Paulista control over the country. The conflict was the largest ever seen in Brazil, with approximately three hundred thousand troops involved. Nearly one hundred thousand Paulistas volunteered to fight the Vargas Administration. This was a popular war, in contrast to 1924, when the Paulista population was untouched and indifferent to the appeals of the army rebels. Failing to make good use of initial advantages, the Paulistas went on the defensive and the fighting reached a stalemate. Peace was negotiated on October 1, 1932, and the revolt ended.[5] No reprisals were taken, and Getúlio Vargas promised to convene a constituent assembly promptly to prepare a new constitution for the country.

Decree Law 22.400, issued in November, 1932, created a committee to prepare a preliminary constitution to be discussed and voted on by a new constituent assembly in 1934.[6] The committee was composed of politicians from Rio Grande do Sul, Minas Gerais and northern Brazil. The group split: One faction favored a fascist-state-oriented constitution granting great social and economic powers; the other, a constitution along more liberal lines of the nineteenth century. Vargas did not demonstrate approval or disapproval of either group, though both attempted to win his favor. He apparently felt it unwise to take a strong stand before all elements were clearly defined.

In 1933 the states began selecting candidates to run for seats in the constituent assembly. In most of the states which had had a one-party system before the 1930 revolution, the same situation existed in 1933. As in pre-1930 Brazil, in the smaller states the government was able, by direct or indirect means, to elect people whom it favored. In São Paulo, Minas Gerais and Rio Grande do Sul, states that had developed some degree of political sophistication before 1930, the contests between opposing party groups were lively. The Interventores managed those in the other states.

The constituent assembly which met early in 1934 consisted of two hundred and fifty representatives from all the states of the country and included fifty delegates from various economic sectors who had the same status as the political representatives. The fifty delegates included deputies for agriculture, industry, commerce, communications and labor. They were chosen through elections by the members of the various economic organizations. The labor delegates were quickly dubbed *pelegos*, or agents of the Ministry of Labor, whose orders they followed closely.

On July 16, 1934, the new Constitution was promulgated. Basically, it was a move toward greater centralization of power in the hands of the national government. The legislative branch sustained the greatest modification, with the Chamber of Deputies made more powerful. In addition to the traditionally elected representatives, the fifty special deputies from the various economic sectors were to have seats in the Chamber. The Senate was reduced in power. The Supreme Court remained basically the same, although it was granted the additional right to declare a law unconstitutional.[7] The presidential office was theoretically stripped of some of its authority and a second term for the President was prohibited. In reality, however, the legislative branch was the docile instrument of a strong chief executive. Anything and everything that Vargas wanted was granted.

The constituent assembly, when it finished work on the Constitution, constituted itself the first regular Congress and elected Vargas President of the Republic for the four-year term 1934 to 1938.

The pace of events in Brazil in the period from mid-1934 to the *coup d'état* of 1937 was swift. The Congress, acting under the pressure of Getúlio Vargas, who saw the political implications and power to be gained by working with labor, enacted social legislation to aid the working class. Labor courts were set up, and some serious attention began to be directed to the problems of lower-income groups in Brazil.

Communist activity increased during the period after the Constitution of 1934 was implemented. Although illegal, the Communist party created a front organization, the National Liberation Alliance, which was under the control of Luís Carlos Prestes. In July, 1935, Vargas outlawed the front organization, but it continued to agitate against the government. In October a strike in northeastern Brazil involving a foreign-owned railroad, the Great Western, was organized by the Alliance and violence resulted. On November 23, the National Liberation Alliance attempted a revolt against the central government. Military units were approached, and the Third Infantry Battalion, with headquarters at Praia Vermelho in Rio de Janeiro, a unit in Rio Grande do Norte and one in Pernambuco joined the rebellion. The revolt did not succeed and was quickly put down. Luís Carlos Prestes and many others were arrested and sentenced to jail.

The rise of a Fascist party was the focus of the next major group opposing the government of Getúlio Vargas. The Integralistas, led by Plínio Salgado and directed by a "council of forty," were an extremely nationalistic, Church-oriented political party that attracted Brazilians by blending Catholicism, mysticism, order and progress, with saluting, green shirt uniforms and parades. With the financial support of the German embassy, the Integralistas actually began to make serious inroads with their appeals to the masses.

In 1937 maneuvering began for the presidential elections that were to be held in the following year. Three candidates seriously sought the presidency and campaigned vigorously. One, José Américo de Almeida, from northeastern Brazil, had briefly been Minister of Public Works. Although a former member of the Vargas cabinet, José Américo was not considered an official candidate of the government. Another candidate was Armando Sales de Oliveira of São Paulo, a popular local political leader. The sheer weight of the Paulista voting population with whatever support could be picked up in other states, in a relatively free election, would probably have given this candidate the election. The third candidate was the leader of the Integralista party, Plínio Salgado, another Paulista, whose campaign was being skillfully managed by San Tiago Dantas and A. Marcondes Filho.[8]

The regime decided not to take a chance on the elections. On November 10, 1937, Vargas, with the support of the armed forces, declared a national emergency, dissolved Congress and took over complete control of the country. A new constitution was proclaimed, molded this time along totalitarian lines. O Estado Novo, the New State, was announced, and Brazil quietly became a dictatorship. The cabinet remained basically the same, and the country calmly went about its business. Over eighty Congressmen went to congratulate Vargas and assure him of their loyalty. Many were later rewarded with administrative positions. The Integralistas applauded the move, expecting to collaborate with Vargas.

Any effective protest to this turn of events had to come from São Paulo, and the efficient deployment of federal troops in the city of São Paulo prevented this. The Paulistas did not want a repeat of 1932, and the remainder of Brazil was inclined to go along with the Vargas *coup*.

General Góes Monteiro gave the following reasons for the *golpe de estado* of November 10. First, he considered the coming presidential elections potentially dangerous to the political stability of the country, since a victorious Paulista candidate might reverse policies adopted by the Vargas Administration. Second, Congress presented a potential threat to the former army rebels, who were now high-ranking officers, as new legislation was being considered which would severely punish officers who led rebellions against the civilian political structure. Third, General Góes Monteiro noted that Interventor Flôres da Cunha of Rio Grande do Sul had broken with Vargas and was attempting to enlist the support of federal troops to carry out a counterrevolution against the central government. Fourth, the Cohen Plan, a terrorist conspiracy of guerrilla activity against the Vargas government, had been uncovered by the secret police. (The charge has been made that this plan never existed and was simply a fabrication by the army to justify the setting up of a dictatorship.) Fifth, General Góes Monteiro claimed that the Integralista party was becoming so strong that they might stage a successful *coup d'etat* against the administration.[9]

Despite these justifications by General Góes Monteiro, the rationale behind the 1937 *coup* is not easily explained and may lie elsewhere. The initial impact of the 1930 revolution had prevented a more serious social and political revolution. The excitement of promised reforms and expected changes had lasted until 1932, but by then there was a feeling that the revolution had run its course and Brazilian politics had returned to its familiar mold. The only significant change brought about by the revolution was that control of the national government had shifted from São Paulo to Rio Grande do Sul. The failure of the São Paulo revolt in July, 1932, saved Rio Grande do Sul from losing mastery of the central government. The successful mobilization of the army by General Góes Monteiro and the apparent unity demonstrated by the other states in support of the Vargas regime during the Paulista revolt gave the Gaúchos a fresh grip on the nation.

Beginning in 1934 with the drafting of the new Constitution, political affairs in Brazil took on an air of unreality. The country was not governed dictatorially, but everyone watched the Vargas Administration cautiously. The influence of the central government was evident in the smaller states, as it had been throughout Brazilian history, but basic economic and social problems were not being solved. As a result of this lack of a successful program on the part of the Vargas team, political extremists from both the left and the right attacked the government for not doing enough to help the people. The uncertainty and aimlessness of the Vargas Administration had been brought out by the 1937 presidential campaign. Apparently General Góes Monteiro acted with the approval of Getúlio Vargas to end this period of indecision. The military had once again saved the political life of Getúlio Vargas. It was clear that the army trusted the Gaúcho politician but did not feel the same way toward the other men who were running for the presidency.

Brazil was governed from 1937 to 1945 by laws that were issued by the executive office, the government again was one man, Getúlio Vargas. Political parties were wiped out by presidential decree on December 2, 1937. Two achievements of the regime were nevertheless to have great impact on contemporary Brazil. The first was the acceleration of the movement toward economic nationalism and the second, the enactment of social legislation.

There has always been a latent feeling in Brazil that the industrial development of the country has been retarded by the operations of foreign investors, especially, after 1930, by United States corporations.[10] An attempt was made in the first year of the Vargas regime to challenge this situation. A Decree Law of December 12, 1930, stated that two-thirds of the labor force of all firms operating in the country must be Brazilian nationals. This law was not enforced very strictly and was amended in 1939 by Decree Law 1843.[11]

Various commissions, councils, departments, institutes and government banks were organized; however, the economic council that was decreed was not created. It was a blend of government planning and free enterprise.

The best example of the mixed corporation in Brazil was the Brazilian national steel company, which took shape in January, 1941. The steel plant at Volta Redonda, which the United States helped finance and install in Brazil, played a great role in pushing the country toward industrialization. The Brazilian army's interest in armament, the social implications that industrialization would bring, considerations of higher standards of living and the Nazi threat were all involved in the decision to start the plant.

After 1937 the focus of the government domestic program was on the urban working-class groups. Provisions in article 137 of the 1937 Constitution included annual holidays with pay, minimum wages, an eight-hour day, social security and medical institutes. Unions were legalized but were kept under close government supervision. Articles 145 to 153 established government control over certain industrial areas that Vargas and his planners considered crucial.

The political implications of these moves are clear, for the growing urban proletariat became one of the supporting pillars of the Vargas Administration. They remained loyal to Vargas even after he had been ousted from office.

In 1938, Vargas eliminated his disillusioned right-wing opponents, the Integralistas, when they made a clumsy and ill-timed attempt to kill him. Entering the presidential residence late at night, the followers of Plínio Salgado fought a running pistol duel with Vargas and his daughter before they were captured.

As the German embassy was linked to the Integralista party, the open admiration that both Vargas and General Góes Monteiro had for the Nazis began to cool. At the same time, Brazilian-American relations began to improve. Osvaldo Aranha, who served as ambassador in Washington and later become Foreign Minister, worked closely with Jefferson Caffery, the United States ambassador in Brazil. Negotiations were worked out in 1940 whereby the Brazilian government granted the United States, first, naval bases in Recife and Bahia and then, shortly after Pearl Harbor, air bases and additional naval installations. Brazil declared war on Germany and Italy in August, 1942, when five Brazilian merchantmen were sunk by German submarines. A Brazilian army later fought in Italy under the command of General Mark Clark.

As the Allies began to win in Europe, the repercussions were felt in Brazil. In April, 1944, Vargas indicated in his usual ambiguous style that the end of the war would perhaps bring free elections to Brazil. In August, 1944, however, Vargas broke temporarily with Osvaldo Aranha, whose enthusiastic endorsement of the United Nations through the Society of Friends of America was considered a potential threat to the political stability of the nation by the military. They feared that the organization might become a rallying point for democratic opponents of the Vargas regime. The army padlocked a meeting hall one night in 1944 when Aranha was to give an important speech, and in protest he resigned from the government.

The year 1945 was the final one of the Vargas dictatorship. It began auspiciously with the arrival of a new American ambassador, a prominent New Dealer, Adolph A. Berle. In February, 1945, the Organization of American States convened a special Inter-American Conference on Problems of War and Peace in Mexico City. By the Act of Chapultepec the member countries adopted the principle that an act of aggression by any nation against an American state would be considered an act of aggression against all. Argentina was not permitted to sign the act until she had declared war on the Axis, and she was admitted to the United Nations only under protest from the Russians. There were unconfirmed rumors that the Russians would not permit Brazil to take a seat in the United Nations unless the country held elections and returned to democratic government. The aim of the Russians was to give as much support as possible to the jailed Communist leader, Luís Carlos Prestes.

Getúlio Vargas stated in February, 1945, that general elections would be held in December of that year to select a new President, Chamber of Deputies and Senate. During the last week in February press censorship was lifted and the Brazilians read a wave of denunciations of the Vargas regime. Political parties began to take shape promptly. The two major parties that appeared were both conservative. The National Democratic Union (União Democrática Nacional; UDN), an urban-based party that contained many wealthy industrialists, selected as its candidate for the presidency Air Brigadier General Eduardo Gomes. The party favored mildly liberal reforms; however, the most prominent men in the party were odd political bedfellows. Sprinkled among the founders were Osvaldo Aranha, Júlio Prestes, President-elect in 1930, former President Artur da Silva Bernardes, Assis Chateaubriand, who controlled the largest newspaper chain in the country, and Francisco Campos, who had written the 1937 Constitution for Vargas.

The other party, the Social Democratic Party (Partido Social Democrático; PSD), inherited the mantle of government. Their candidate was Getúlio Vargas' Minister of War, Eurico Gaspar Dutra. The PSD had strength in São Paulo, Minas Gerais and Rio Grande do Sul, and its position in the smaller states was unassailable where the government was the major political force. In the northeast and the interior, the traditional rural aristocrats had either collaborated closely with the Vargas machine or had been forced out of politics.

A third, smaller party organized by the government was called the Brazilian Labor party (Partido Trabalhista Brasileiro; PTB), in which the official unions worked closely with the Minister of Labor. They began to demand that Vargas remain as dictator of the country. Within the Labor party and at the same time directly responsible to Vargas was a small but vocal group which became known as Queremistas (We want Vargas).

Other parties began to appear but none was to have the congressional strength of the three mentioned. In April, 1945, the Communist leader, Luís Carlos Prestes, was released from prison and promptly backed Getúlio Vargas, calling him a great democrat. Vargas had apparently worked out a *modus vivendi* with Prestes in true Brazilian style. The army watched uneasily as the Communist party was permitted to function and began to organize for the coming election.

In September, 1945, as the December election date drew closer, there was some apprehension that Vargas might organize a *coup d'état* similar to that of November, 1937. When Vargas replaced the chief of police of Rio de Janeiro with his disreputable brother Benjamin Vargas, suspicion grew in army circles that it was just a question of time until Vargas would announce that he was staying on.

The American embassy apparently learned details of a Vargas plot to call off the elections and stay in power. Ambassador Berle made an extremely pointed speech in which he declared: "Public opinion has rejoiced over the steady Brazilian determination to develop and use the institution of democratic government, and has acclaimed the steps taken by the Brazilian government to reach the goal of constitutional democracy. The pledge of free Brazilian elections set for a definite date, by a government whose word the United States has found inviolable, has been hailed with as much satisfaction in the United States as in Brazil itself." The speech was delivered to an audience of UDN political leaders.[12]

Vargas may have been watching the events in Argentina. There Juan Perón had been imprisoned by the army, and Evita, his wife, called out the packing-house workers to free him (October 9 to 17, 1945). At precisely the same time, Vargas was maneuvering in Brazil and receiving reports concerning the successful use of labor unions by Perón to thwart the Argentine military, from his close Gaúcho friend, Batista Luzardo, who was serving as ambassador in Argentina.

Worried Brazilian military men watched Vargas uneasily. General Góes Monteiro met with General Eurico Dutra and Brigadier General Eduardo Gomes, and all agreed that Vargas might be attempting a move that would halt elections and perhaps endanger the military establishment. The decision was reached to end the Vargas reign and install the Chief Justice of the Supreme Court as temporary head of the government until elections were held in December. To prevent Vargas from outmaneuvering them, they acted quickly. On October 17 teletype messages were sent by General Góes Monteiro to all commands—and tanks rumbled out to take positions around the presidential palace. The army had moved and Vargas had fallen. In typical Brazilian style Vargas retired peacefully to his ranch in São Borja in southern Brazil. The circle had closed. Vargas had returned to his native home.

What had the fifteen years meant to Brazil? No one could turn the clock back. Brazil would never return to her pre-1930 condition, either politically or economically. Yet the Vargas period is not all black and white.

From the political perspective, Brazil had both suffered and benefited. It suffered in that fifteen years of political education had been denied to the Brazilian electorate. The give and take of a democratic society is not easily learned, and the Brazilians were slowly edging toward more and more participation in politics from the inception of the republic in 1889 to the 1930 election. But for fifteen years decisions were made for the Brazilians, and a generation grew up without having voted or heard opposition politicians argue positions. Political parties had to develop and build followings. But more important, a deep sense of cynicism regarding politicians developed in the fifteen years that the Vargas men controlled the government. Though Getúlio Vargas may not have enriched himself, there is no question that the men around him amassed fortunes and used their power to give favors to others. Personal relationships were more important than the laws of the nation. A vast network of economic and political power relationships developed which caused havoc and disrupted political life from 1945 to 1965.

Brazilians had benefited politically in that there existed in 1945 a pluralistic power base unintentionally provided by the Vargas dictatorship. Bringing the working class into the political arena, Getúlio Vargas had accomplished what the Argentine governing class was unable or unprepared to do. In the urban centers the Brazilian working class was able to make the transition to participation in the political activities of the country without violence. The Vargas regime had permitted and encouraged the maturation of that sector of society, so that when the country returned to democratic procedures, labor took a role in the give and take of everyday politics and received benefits from the political structure. The lower-income groups in Brazil were not systematically excluded as they were in other Latin American countries. Nor did they have to tear their demands from the government through bloody power struggles, as occurred in Mexico, Cuba and Colombia. The government in Brazil during the dictatorship and the period following was not an enemy of the working class, but a government that responded somewhat to its demands. During the dictatorship it had been a benevolent leader; in the period that followed, pressure through balloting and other organized maneuvers was sufficient. Whether this type of development would have been permitted or encouraged by the Paulista elite is an open-ended question.

Another benefit of the Vargas period was the temporary breaking of the dominance of the state of São Paulo over the rest of the country. For too long the fortunes of Brazil had been determined by the interests of this very powerful and important state. What was good for São Paulo was good for the remainder of Brazil. Sometimes this may have been true; often it was not. Often Paulista businessmen made the north of Brazil their own type of colony. The north and northeast were secure markets and also the source of raw materials for southern Brazil. The Vargas period to a slight degree dislodged the complete power control of São Paulo over the country.

Credit should be given to Getúlio Vargas for his conscious attempt to break down the strong regional sentiments that existed before 1930, for Brazil during the Vargas period became more of a unified nation. Regionalism still existed, to be sure, and exists today in Brazil; but for the first time in modern Brazilian history a chief of state had spoken to Brazilians from a non-Paulista base.

Thus, the Vargas epoch was a mixture of gains and benefits in some sectors, setbacks and negative results in others. Nevertheless, by comparison with other Latin American countries during the same time span, in Brazil the era was one of economic and social progress and continuous development.

Chapter 7

The Search for Stability: 1945 to 1966

Brazilian political history from October, 1945 to March, 1964, made a complete cycle. In 1945 the army deposed Getúlio Vargas and turned over the political affairs of the nation to civilian leaders. For nineteen years the generals played a subtle but secondary role in national affairs. In March, 1964, the army stepped forward again and deposed the João Goulart Administration. A cowed Congress installed General Humberto de Alencar Castelo Branco as the chief executive, and the military became the most important force in the Brazilian political process.

A few days after the successful Octobor 17, 1945, revolution, the army made Supreme Court Chief José Linhares acting President, to rule until the elections were held and the new chief executive was inaugurated. The political parties, reassured by the army, continued their campaign, and elections were held as scheduled on December 2, 1945. The only new element that had been added to the Brazilian political scene was the Communist party's last-minute decision to present a presidential candidate of its own.

Getúlio Vargas, before his abrupt departure, indicated that of the two generals running for the presidency he preferred Eurico Gaspar Dutra. This, plus PSD control of many of the smaller states, transformed this group into a semiofficial government party and was enough to give General Dutra the presidency.

Eurico Gaspar Dutra	PSD (Social Democratic party)	3,251,507
Eduardo Gomes	UDN (National Democratic Union)	2,039,341
Iêdo Fiuza	PCB (Communist party of Brazil)	569,818

General Dutra was peacefully inaugurated in January, 1946. The one cloud on the horizon of the new democratic state was the size of the Communist party vote.

In Congress the PSD emerged as the most powerful party, followed closely by the UDN. The third ranking party was the PTB. This ratio held for about eighteen years. Only in 1963 did the PTB briefly become the most important party in the Brazilian Congress.

One of the first tasks of the government was to draw up a new constitution. When Congress convened in February, 1946, it met as a constitutional convention and set to work preparing the document, which was finished in September, 1946.

From a political point of view the 1946 Constitution preserved the traditional separation of powers among the executive, legislative and judicial branches of the government. Though it returned to the older type of liberalism found in the 1934 and 1891 Constitutions, the new document did retain many of the articles found in the 1937 Constitution, especially those in the area of economic and social legislation. Much was drawn from the 1917 Mexican Constitution and the German Weimar Republic Constitution of 1919. Many parts of the new document were obviously designed to continue Brazilian economic nationalism, which had developed and flourished during the Vargas period. There was a preoccupation with abuses of economic power, and Article 148 is a combination of the Sherman Anti-Trust Law and regulations of the Federal Trade Commission in the United States. Other sections contain detailed labor statements, and the right to strike is recognized.[1]

Any understanding of the constitutional and political life in Brazil must spring from the idea that Brazil before and during most of the Vargas period functioned basically under an executive form of government. Much of the power and most of the decisions were in the hands of the chief executive. The only possible check was that of the military. Throughout the old republic (1889 to 1930) there was no previous experience of a strong legislative branch giving direction to the government, nor was there any tradition of a vigorous independent judiciary. What existed in the previous Brazilian scene and exists today is executive government. The shape, the form, the style of the government in Brazil is always set by the chief executive.

The power of the national government in directing the affairs of the smaller units of the Brazilian federation depends on the President's use of his power; however, he is restricted in his control over the more sophisticated and economically powerful states of São Paulo, Minas Gerais, Rio Grande do Sul and the city of Rio de Janeiro, which since 1960 has been known as the state of Guanabara. But in the other states, executive power operating through various channels makes itself felt.

The Dutra Administration, from 1946 to 1951, was a relatively calm and progressive one for the country. Considering the fact that Brazil was timidly experimenting with democracy for the first time since 1930 and that the Brazilian electorate was learning new skills, the results were encouraging.

In the 1947 congressional elections, however, the Communist party broke in to challenge the PSD, UDN and PTB parties, which had carved up congressional representation among them. Receiving approximately 16 per cent of the total vote cast in 1947, the Communists picked up one Senate seat and fifteen in the Chamber of Deputies, and appeared to be gaining in popularity. Fear of the Communists by the Catholic Church and other political parties resulted in pressure on President Dutra's Administration, which moved against the Communist party on the grounds that it was an agent of a foreign government. In May, 1947, the Communist party was declared illegal and once again went underground. The following year the Congress voted to strip the elected representatives of the party of their posts in the legislature.

Eurico Gaspar Dutra gave Brazil a fairly decent administration, but he demonstrated no great executive leadership. After fifteen years of dictatorship, his most important role was to see that the country's political procedures got off to a successful start. This he did. He could not control the deteriorating economic conditions of the country, nor could he manage the postwar inflation that had developed. But President Dutra must be given credit for pulling the Brazilian state through the first five perilous years after the dictatorship.

In 1950, pending new presidential elections, three candidates threw their hats into the ring. Dutra was then attacked from both the left and the right. The most dangerous attacks, however, came from Getúlio Vargas—who had broken with Dutra and was now a senator from Rio Grande do Sul—and from the outlawed Communist party, charging Dutra with being a tool of the United States.

The Dutra Administration and the PSD sponsored Cristiano Machado, governor of the powerful state of Minas Gerais. The UDN candidate once again was Brigadier General Eduardo Gomes. The relative lack of enthusiasm with which the Brazilians had received and accepted the Dutra Administration and the PSD party forecast a victory for the UDN. Many felt that the turn of the opposition had come and that Brigadier General Gomes and the UDN would be elected. However, a new dimension was added to the scene when Getúlio Vargas announced his candidacy.

Getúlio Vargas announced that he would run for the presidency on the Labor party ticket (PTB). His running mate was João Café Filho, who was from northeastern Brazil and a member of the Social Progressive party (Partido Social Progressista; PSP). The PSP was the personal vehicle of São Paulo politician Ademar de Barros.

The contest was between Vargas and Gomes. The official candidate of the government, Cristiano Machado, was soon forgotten. In the interior of Brazil, in the small towns and villages, in the smaller states, the citizens who were just entering the political process knew that the name of Getúlio Vargas was magic. Vargas was Brazil to these people and the opportunity to vote for this man, who apparently had done so much for them during the 1930 to 1945 period, could not be resisted. In many parts of the country where local political machines took great pains to increase the number of registered voters by teaching the illiterate citizens to sign their names, the result came out contrary to what had been anticipated. Many of the new voters struck an independent stance and voted for Vargas and the PTB rather than the PSD candidate or the UDN General.

The working-class urban vote, plus the unconditional regional vote from Rio Grande do Sul, were enough to give Vargas the presidency in 1950.

Getúlio Vargas	PTD	3,849,000
Eduardo Gomes	UDN	2,342,384
Cristiano Machado	PSD	1,697,193

Vargas was inaugurated in January, and most of his old team returned, but the years were not happy ones for the former dictator. The old Vargas touch seemed to have disappeared. Vargas did not have a Congress that he could control as he had from 1934 to 1937, nor the powers of a dictator. The composition of Congress had continued the three major blocs, the PSD, the PTB and the UDN. Occasionally Vargas was able to bring together an uneasy coalition of the PSD and the PTB for legislative purposes, but this unity did not last for long periods.

Economic problems plagued the Vargas regime, and graft and corruption began to engulf the Administration. Many of these features had existed during the Vargas dictatorship, but at that time there was no free press to expose or comment on them. Despite criticism, Vargas continued to govern with the men of 1930. Góes Monteiro was Minister of War; Osvaldo Aranha was Minister of Finance; João Neves da Fontoura was Foreign Minister. To many it appeared that Vargas was rerunning the 1930 to 1945 period. There was one notable exception. Vargas selected as his Minister of Labor a young politician from Rio Grande do Sul, João Goulart, and appeared to be training him as the heir-apparent.

Labor Minister Goulart held office from August, 1953, to February, 1954; he worked closely with left-wing elements in labor and became temporarily popular with the workers by pushing for higher minimum wages. His action, however, served to increase opposition from the military to the Vargas Administration and ultimately brought about its downfall.

Events in Brazil reached a climax in August, 1954, when a newspaper editor, Carlos Lacerda, who had been exposing graft and corruption around the President, was the victim of an assassination attempt by one of Getúlio Vargas' personal bodyguards.[2] Lacerda was wounded and his aide, a major in the air force, was killed. Charges were made in the press that Vargas was directly implicated, and various sectors of the military began to act independently of the President to bring the culprit to justice.[3] A number of top-ranking military officials signed a manifesto requesting that Getúlio Vargas resign from the presidency. Most of the armed forces supported this action.[4] There was unity among the top military officials, who agreed that Vargas should step down from the presidency and turn over the position to his Vice-President, João Café Filho.

There is both irony and pathos in the events. Getúlio Vargas had ruled for fifteen years with the support of the military forces. In 1945 he had left the executive office when the military demanded that he retire. Now legally elected President by the voters of the country, he was being forced to resign by groups that he had formerly relied upon and used during his dictatorship period. Vargas, rather than resign, committed suicide on August 24, 1954, leaving two notes which have been the focus of considerable political controversy. The first, a handwritten and signed note, simply declared, "To the wrath of my enemies I leave the legacy of my death. I carry with me the sorrow of not having been able to do for the humble all that I desired. Getúlio Vargas." The second was a typewritten political manifesto which indirectly charged that international economic interests had taken vasts profits from the country and thus were responsible for the bad economic conditions in Brazil, and also by implication for his decision to take his own life. Both the political style and tone of the manifesto tend to conflict with the previous pronouncements of Getúlio Vargas; however, there is little doubt that Vargas always had reservations concerning the role foreign capital should play in Brazil. The cutting down of United States financial aid during his presidency may have been partially responsible for the sentiments expressed in the manifesto, which has become a rallying point for ultra-nationalists in Brazil.[5]

The Brazilian reaction to the suicide was not violent. Most Brazilians were mystified and, though the army was mobilized for mob violence, with the exception of rioting in Pôrto Alegre, capital of Vargas' home state, Rio Grande do Sul, the nation remained calm. Café Filho moved up to the presidency to serve out the remaining year of Vargas' term, while preparations continued for the presidential election of 1955.

Two of the major parties, the PSD and the PTB, joined to support Juscelino Kubitschek, governor of the state of Minas Gerais, for the presidency. His opponents were Juarez Távora of the UDN party and Paulista Ademar de Barros. General Távora was one of the few men who, though from the northeastern part of Brazil, had a national reputation and was respected throughout the country. Generally, to win the election in the post-Getúlio Vargas period a presidential candiate had to have one large and popular state behind him to insure victory, as Brazilians are still extremely state conscious.

Juscelino Kubitschek could count solidly on the Minas Gerais vote and Ademar de Barros on the São Paulo voters, thus making it necessary for Juarez Távora to run strongly throughout the nation to counterbalance the power of the two most populous states in the union. It was a relatively close election.

Juscelino Kubitschek	PSD-PTB	3,077,411
Juarez Távora	UDN	2,610,462
Ademar de Barros	PSP	2,222,725

The election was interpreted by many as a victory and revindication of the Vargas forces, especially when the vice-presidency was won by João Goulart, former Minister of Labor, who ran on the labor ticket along with Kubitschek.

After the election a political crisis occurred. Rumors began to circulate that men in the Café Filho Administration would not permit President-elect Kubitschek and Vice-President-elect Goulart to take office in January of 1956. Tension heightened when President Café Filho suffered a heart attack and took a leave of absence on November 8, 1955. According to Brazilian constitutional law, Café Filho turned over the presidency to the Speaker of the Chamber of Deputies, Carlos Luz. Since he was taking the presidency only temporarily, Luz was expected to continue the Café Filho cabinet; however, a controversy had developed between Carlos Luz and the Minister of War, Henrique Lott. Carlos Luz requested that Lott resign and issued the order removing the Minister of War on November 11.

At this, the pro-Vargas forces grouped around War Minister Lott, and President-elect Kubitschek went into action, fearing that the Administration, now composed of anti-Vargas forces, was going to proceed with a *coup d'état* and prevent him from taking office. There is much conjecture in this area, but the hard facts are that Minister of War Lott rejected his dismissal and sent tanks into the streets. Luz alerted many political leaders who believed as he did that the pro-Vargas forces were executing a *coup d'état,* and fled to the open seas aboard a Brazilian battleship.[6]

Once on the high seas, Luz issued a manifesto explaining his action. The Brazilian Congress convened and refused to accept his explanation of events, and in a joint session declared that Carlos Luz had violated the Constitution. It appointed President Pro Tem of the Senate Artur Ramos to head the Brazilian government temporarily until Juscelino Kubitschek could be inaugurated. Receiving word of the action, Carlos Luz ordered the battleship to return to port. Amidst charges and countercharges, Artur Ramos held the reins of government until the inauguration of Juscelino Kubitschek in January, 1956. The Minister of War for the entire period of the Kubitschek Administration (1956–1961) was General Henrique Lott.

Politics during the Kubitschek Administration had an air of unreality. The President promised to give Brazil fifty years of progress in five. Among his goals were road construction, the building of Brasília, the new capital of the country, seven hundred miles in the interior, and the creation of an automobile industry. Along with the realization of many of these projects came tremendous inflation in Brazil. Graft and mismanagement reached astounding proportions even for Brazil, but since most Brazilians participated in this great political barbecue, no dangerous trouble zones developed, except possibly in the Brazilian northeast. Though inflation was robbing much of the middle class, at the end of the Administration in 1960 the middle class had more wealth than in 1955 and an air of optimism prevailed.

The 1960 presidential election accurately reflected Brazilian democratic development. Three major candidates represented three different currents present in Brazil at that time. Jânio Quadros, governor of the state of São Paulo, represented a reform mood of the people. A political maverick, Quadros did not belong to any of the three major parties. Throughout his meteoric political career in the state of São Paulo he had drawn support from smaller, insignificant parties and had won victory after victory on a personal plane, not on a party basis. Rising from an obscure city councilman to mayor in the city of São Paulo and then to governor of the state, Jânio Quadros had built up a reputation as a reformer and a man who got things done.[7]

After long debate the UDN decided to support Jânio Quadros for the presidency. The joining of Quadros and the UDN was advantageous to both. Quadros needed the organizational support of the UDN in the smaller and less politically sophisticated regions of Brazil, where he was not well known. There were still areas where the machine was essential for election victories. The party stood to gain, for it had no political leader within its ranks who could win the presidency.

Opposing Jânio Quadros was the quasi-official candidate of the government, General Henrique Lott, Minister of War and the strong man behind the presidency of Juscelino Kubitschek. The PSD and the PTB made an uneasy alliance to support Lott, with João Goulart for the vice-presidency. General Lott was conservative and predictable, and it was assumed he would continue the program of the previous administration.

The third major candidate was Ademar de Barros, also a former governor of the state of São Paulo, who was in control of the PSP and had strong support in the state of São Paulo, the suburbs of Rio de Janeiro and a few small northeastern states.

All candidates added to the political development of the country by campaigning vigorously all over Brazil. The focus was the southeast, where the greatest literacy and largest number of voters were to be found. The state of São Paulo witnessed the candidates visiting every hamlet and town. Minas Gerais was another target. Rio de Janeiro and Pôrto Alegre were both host to the candidates. Even the northeast and the remote Amazon area for the first time were exposed to presidential campaign speeches. Every twentieth-century technique of political campaigning was brought into play, through television, radio, newspapers and personal appearances. The 1960 campaign did a great deal to make Brazil feel, act and think as a nation.

The relatively open political structure of Brazil is illustrated by the fact that the semi-official government candidate held the highest rank in the armed forces and was supported by two of the major parties, and yet lost the election. This combination of political power would be impressive in any country, and in a young developing democracy like Brazil, only fifteen years out from under dictatorship, it indicates that some degree of sophistication and democratic procedures had developed.

The election was a smashing victory for Jânio Quadros. The Brazilians had apparently found a political leader who was not symbolic of any one state but represented the nation. The image that he projected was one of reform and a clearing up of the muddle of federal affairs. The voting statistics contain interesting and valuable clues to future political developments.

Jânio Quadros	UDN	5,636,623
Henrique Lott	PSD-PTB	3,846,825
Ademar de Barros	PSP	2,195,709

Approximately eleven million Brazilians cast votes for a presidential candidate in 1960, and Quadros won in every one of the major states. This had rarely happened in Brazilian political history and indicated how national was his victory.

São Paulo:

Quadros	1,588,593
Lott	441,755
Barros	855,093

Minas Gerais:

Quadros	692,044
Lott	679,951
Barros	183,599

Rio Grande do Sul:

Quadros	541,031
Lott	431,497
Barros	214,963

Guanabara (City of Rio de Janeiro):

Quadros	418,813
Lott	287,836
Barros	250,117

Tremendous enthusiasm greeted the inauguration of Jânio Quadros. Brazil seemed poised on the threshold of a new era. The political atmosphere crackled with excitement, and everyone was prepared to follow the President and make any sacrifices that were demanded. The President took up residence in Brasília, the new location of the federal government, and the nation waited for the reforms. They were, however, not forthcoming.

Jânio Quadros did not have a strong operational base in the Congress. The major parties were still the big three, PSD, UDN and PTB. The PTB and PSD combined had roughly one hundred eighty-two seats in the Chamber of Deputies; whereas the UDN and all the other smaller parties that could be counted on in any crucial question amounted to one hundred seven. Ademar de Barros (PSP) had approximately twenty-five deputies who followed his orientation. In the Senate a similar situation existed. Quadros could count on nineteen senators; whereas opposition groups had thirty-four. A few senators followed Ademar de Barros' PSP.[8]

President Quadros apparently could not govern the country with this type of Congress. Instead he embarked on a program of personal contacts with the various state governors, built up close liaisons between the various state entities and the national government and thus bypassed the national Congress. Criticism began to develop, and when Quadros began to act erratically by cutting himself off from his own cabinet ministers, a crisis began to develop. Late in August, 1961, Jânio incurred the wrath of many sectors in Brazil by granting the nation's highest military honor to Ché Guevara, an Argentine revolutionary who was one of the top leaders of the Fidel Castro Cuban government. The move by Quadros was obviously a grandstand attempt to provoke the United States. As previous Cuban-Brazilian relations had never been close, this action by President Quadros was considered a calculated political maneuver.

Also late in August, 1961, only seven months after taking office, President Quadros approached a number of state governors in an attempt to win their support for an extra-legal concentration of power in the hands of the chief executive. One of the governors approached, Carlos Lacerda of Guanabara, denounced the President on a television broadcast. Shortly after this, on August 25, President Quadros decided to resign. He called in the officers of the armed services and explained that he could not govern Brazil because of congressional opposition, and was resigning. The top military officials pleaded with Quadros not to resign, for political house cleaning had begun for the first time since 1930.

President Quadros refused, insisted that his letter of resignation was irrevocable and ordered that it be delivered to the Chamber of Deputies. Jânio Quadros had twice before used the technique of threatened resignation to achieve political ends, and it should have worked again in 1961.[9] That it failed is attributable to a number of precise causes.

First, Congress acted immediately to accept his resignation.

Second, the armed forces would not back up Quadros in his vague move to take over complete power in Brazil.

Third, the mass of the population, though still enthusiastic toward Quadros, did not protest in the major cities, where organized protest must start to be effective. The resignation of Quadros in either São Paulo or Rio de Janeiro might have triggered dangerous mass demonstrations. But Brasília is nearly seven hundred miles from these cities, and tendering his resignation in Brasília, Quadros acted in a vacuum. The people learned about the event only after it was all over.

A fourth point is a conjectural one: that Quadros never expected his secretary to deliver the resignation letter.

Quadros left a train of confusion and uneasiness behind him as he went into self-imposed exile in England. His single capricious act of resignation did more harm to the nation than the entire Vargas period. It smashed the self-confidence of the Brazilian electorate and brought down the whole fabric of the Brazilian political structure.

According to the 1946 Constitution, the Vice-President automatically assumed the presidency. Vice-President João Goulart was, however, unacceptable to the top commanders of the armed forces. In the short time President Quadros had held office, he had permitted the militant wing of the armed forces, those unalterably opposed to Vargas and Goulart, to take control of the nation's military establishment. To make matters worse, the precise moment of Quadros' resignation, Goulart was in Red China on a trade mission, having been sent there by the President. Informed of Quadros' resignation, Goulart started for Brazil, deliberately taking a slow and circuitous route, hoping for the political air to clear before he returned.

The heads of the armed forces, meeting with field officers in Brasília, São Paulo and Rio de Janeiro, agreed to take matters into their own hands and keep Goulart from assuming the presidency. The Minister of War, Odílio Denís, speaking for all the branches of the military, stated that Goulart was a threat to democratic government and that his control of the executive branch of the government would mean the return of the corrupt Vargas political apparatus. The military chiefs of staff threatened to arrest Goulart the moment he landed on Brazilian soil. It appeared that the Vice-President would not take office, when, for the first time in Brazilian history, the unity of the military forces was shattered.

The split occurred when General José Machado Lopes, chief of the third federal military district based in Pôrto Alegre and covering the state of Rio Grande do Sul, issued a public statement declaring that he would obey the Constitution of 1946, which called for the installation of João Goulart as president. By making this statement, General Lopes implied that he would not obey orders of the Minister of War, who was leading the opposition to Goulart.

Civil war seemed imminent as armored divisions from the second military district began to ring the state of Rio Grande do Sul. This type of situation had never occurred before in Brazil. The only previous situation resembling it was the 1932 São Paulo rebellion. The 1961 Gaúcho rebellion threatened to be more violent and bloody, as the governor of Rio Grande do Sul was Goulart's brother-in-law, Leonel Brizola. The Governor, a wealthy rancher and demagogue, had made unequivocal statements that the presidency legally should be in João Goulart's hands, and that any action to prevent Goulart from taking office was a violation of the Constitution. The mass of the population of Rio Grande do Sul was solidly behind him in this attitude. It was a blend of constitutionalism and regionalism as well as a family affair. The citizens of Pôrto Alegre were given rifles by the state government and were ready for civil war.

The Minister of War wavered as popular opposition to his stand also appeared in Brasília. In the nation's capital, the acting President of Brazil, Ranieri Mazzilli, the Speaker of the Chamber of Deputies, faced an angry and confused Congress that regarded Goulart as the legal President. The legislative branch was also unhappy with the military for having intervened so blatantly in constitutional political procedures. The impasse between Congress and the army was broken with a compromise plan, whereby Goulart would take over the presidential office but theoretically would be stripped of his powers. A constitutional amendment was proposed and accepted by Congress, giving Brazil a parliamentary government with a President and a Prime Minister.

The commanding generals of the armed forces in Brasília accepted this formula rather than risk a civil war with federal units opposing each other. Another important factor in the military decision was the lack of solid public support for their anti-Goulart position.

Article XX added to the 1946 Constitution gave increased powers to a Prime Minister responsible to the Brazilian Congress. All legislative acts were to be signed by the Prime Minister, countersigned by the cabinet minister most concerned with the legislation and finally signed by the President. In a country that was having trouble getting any legislation through Congress, this new system meant utter chaos.

But civil war had been averted, and Goulart went from Rio Grande do Sul to Brasília, where he was installed as the first parliamentary President of Brazil. This system of government lasted for sixteen months, from September, 1961, to January, 1963, when in a national plebescite the people voted to return to the presidential form of government.

In practical terms, Brazil had no national government during these sixteen months. Three men served as Prime Minister: Tancredo Neves, Francisco de Paulo Brochado da Rocha and Hermes Lima. The political picture was confused and the country drifted toward anarchy. President Goulart, an inept administrator hampered by the new constitutional amendment which pared down the effectiveness of the executive office, could do nothing to prevent the chaos that developed.

Adding further to the problems of the period was the fragmented nature of Congress. The Brazilian legislature failed to maintain any party discipline and was unable to direct the country. The Chamber of Deputies up to September, 1962, contained three hundred twenty-six members distributed among the following parties:

PSD (Social Democratic party)	116
PTB (Brazilian Labor party)	66
UDN (National Democratic Union)	66
PSP (Social Progressive party)	25
PR (Republican party)	16
PDC (Christian Democratic party)	8
PSB (Brazilian Socialist party)	8
PTN (National Workers party)	6
PL (Liberation party)	5
PRP (Popular Representation party)	3
PST (Social Workers party)	1
No Party	6

The September, 1962, Senate breakdown revealed the following:

PSD (Social Democratic party)	20
UDN (National Democratic Union)	19

PTB (Brazilian Labor party)	15
PL (Liberation party)	3
PR (Republican party)	1
PSP (Social Progressive party)	1
PTN (National Workers party)	1

These figures do not provide a true picture of the power concentration by party. Because of the outlandish location of the national capital congressional sessions were poorly attended, and it was extremely difficult to obtain quorums. Brasília is a daring and beautiful experiment in architecture and city planning, but from a political point of view it is dangerous. The problem of keeping congressmen at work in Washington was magnified a thousand times in the interior of Brazil.

Another factor that rendered these congressional statistics deceptive was the lack of party discipline. Rarely were party lines observed in the voting. On important issues, members crossed party lines and voted according to the special circumstances surrounding their own political operations.

The returns in the congressional and gubernatorial elections of October, 1962, were regional responses to special problems faced in each area. In São Paulo, former President Jânio Quadros attempted to return to power by running for governor of the state. When Quadros returned to Brazil after his self-imposed exile, there was no question that he would win the election, for he was genuinely popular, and the people were simply waiting for the real explanation as to why Quadros had been "forced" out of the presidency. Most of Quadros' supporters were sure that he had not resigned of his own free will, but when he failed in his promise to tell in detail about the mysterious forces that had pressured him into resigning in August, 1961, the Paulista electorate gave up waiting for the explanation and demonstrated their disenchantment at the polls. In a very tight race in October, 1962, Quadros lost the governorship to Ademar de Barros by a vote of 1,249,000 to 1,125,941.[10] The political parties were insignificant in this particular election. Paulistas were voting for personalities. The voting edge for Jânio Quadros in the urban working-class districts of São Paulo was only about 4 per cent over that of Ademar de Barros, but the well-financed and smoothly functioning Ademar de Barros machine was unbeatable in the interior. His victory proved conclusively his skill and political ability and the effectiveness of his political organization. It also indicated to some degree the relatively conservative nature of the São Paulo voter.

In another part of Brazil, Pernambuco governor-elect Miguel Arrais demonstrated that the northeast of Brazil was in a different situation and seeking more dramatic solutions to its problems. Miguel Arrais had campaigned on a platform that promised alleviation of the grinding poverty in his region and openly accepted the support of many Marxist groups.

With the October, 1962, elections out of the way, attention returned to the executive office and the activities of President João Goulart. The President went to the nation in an apparent appeal to establish a new political power structure. The parliamentary system was not working, and the Prime Minister had become a simple servant of the President. Goulart felt that the Brazilians should be given a chance to vote on continuing the parliamentary system or returning the political machinery of the country to the presidential form. He charged that the chaos, administrative collapse, inflation and drift of Brazilian national life was caused exclusively by the parliamentary system. In the plebescite held in January, 1963, the vote indicated clearly that the citizens were unhappy with the political situation and wanted a change. If power in the hands of President Goulart would improve the political situation, the Brazilians were willing to grant it to him. Thus Brazil returned to an executive form of government, which lasted from January, 1963, to March, 1964.

The political tragedy of the country from the restoration of presidential power to the revolution of 1964 is sharply etched. João Goulart turned out to be one of the most incompetent and blundering politicians to have appeared on the Brazilian national scene in fifty years. Instead of consolidating the disunited political forces and building a political consensus, Goulart succeeded in further fragmenting the left and at the same uniting the middle and right sectors into a solid opposition front. The steps are clearly marked.

Badly shaken by the defections of the federal military district in Rio Grande do Sul in support of Goulart in August, 1961, the army general staff proceeded cautiously to reknit the solidarity of the top-ranking generals in opposition to the President. João Goulart aided this process by his mild reaction when a revolt of air force sergeants in Brasília was suppressed in September, 1963. A shiver of apprehension went through the entire officer corps of the Brazilian armed forces, when it became apparent that President Goulart was attempting to build a political power base among the noncommissioned officers to counterbalance his suspicion and distrust of the officers. He thus succeeded in reuniting the leaders of the armed forces into a solid anti-Goulart group.

Directly beneath the military in the political power structure of Brazil were the four rich and dynamic states of São Paulo, Minas Gerais, Rio Grande do Sul and the new state of Guanabara, formerly the Federal District, Rio de Janeiro. The executive office always needed these states to govern effectively, and in 1963 João Goulart needed them more than they needed the President. In the 1962 gubernatorial elections Governor Leonel Brizola's candidate to succeed him in the governorship of Rio Grande do Sul had lost, and the state machinery was in the hands of anti-Administration forces. Governor Magalhães Pinto of Minas Gerais broke with the President when federal funds were cut off from the state. In São Paulo, Governor Ademar de Barros ignored the President completely. Finally, in Guanabara, Governor Carlos Lacerda was in open political warfare with the President. The executive office, in an attempt to bring chaos to the city of Rio de Janeiro and force Lacerda out, blocked food shipments, creating artificial shortages and resulting in food riots. The Rio de Janeiro fire department was federalized, thus removing it from Governor Lacerda's control and creating more uneasiness in the tense city. The President made frequent trips to Rio de Janeiro and demanded military cover while he gave inflammatory speeches to the working classes.

The final blow to presidential prestige came when his own political party, the PTB, joined the PSD and the UDN in refusing to grant the temporary state-of-siege powers that Goulart requested. With the military, the major states and the political parties all in opposition to the President, his fate was sealed.

In an attempt to break the circle being drawn around him, President Goulart tried to create a new political power structure. Disregarding the warnings of many of his political advisers, Goulart invited Governor Miguel Arrais of Pernambuco and brother-in-law Leonel Brizola, now a congressman from the state of Guanabara, to join him in an appeal directed exclusively to the lower-income groups of the nation. A series of widely publicized mass rallies was held and in Rio de Janeiro on March 13, 1964, President Goulart further threatened to adjourn Congress, offered the right to vote to the illiterate population and dramatically signed an executive decree expropriating large tracts of land for an agrarian reform program.[11]

On March 31, 1964, as the political structure was on the verge of collapse, the military and the major state governors, correctly gauging the state of public opinion, moved to bring an end to the political nightmare and administrative chaos that had engulfed the nation. In three drama-filled days the commanders of the First, Second and Third Armies coordinated their plans with Governor Magalhães Pinto of Minas Gerais, Governor Ademar de Barros of São Paulo, Governor Carlos Lacerda of Guanabara and Governor Ildo Meneghetti of Rio Grande do Sul. President Goulart could not mobilize any important sector of the nation to defend his regime. Labor unions, rural workers, the Church, Congress and all the political parties distrusted him. He fled the country unmourned and discredited.

Though the revolt against President Goulart was a genuinely popular one, the Brazilian army participation was the single most important element in the eventual success or failure of the movement. Thus, after the revolt, the military men moved quickly to make sure they did not lose control of the revolution. They first dictated Institutional Act Number One, which amended the 1946 Constitution to permit Congress to elect General Humberto Castelo Branco, one of the leaders of the rebellion, to the presidency.[12] He was to serve until 1966 but when it became apparent that this period was too short to carry out the planned reforms his term of office was extended to March, 1967.

In a sweeping move against allies, both real and suspected, of deposed President Goulart, the army quickly jailed thousands of citizens. Over four hundred politicians were stripped of their political rights, among then former President Jânio Quadros, Juscelino Kubitschek and João Goulart. Kubitschek was permitted to go into voluntary exile. Congress sanctioned all these moves, and the country began to function with tight military control of the political system. Though the 1946 Constitution had been theoretically maintained, in reality the military governed through Institutional Act Number One.

The army-dominated government of Castelo Branco attempted, in the period from April, 1964, to October, 1965, to work within some framework of legality. The Supreme Court was respected, Congress heeded the suggestions of the President and passed much-needed reform legislation and political parties functioned.

For eighteen months President Castelo Branco projected the image of a competent chief executive who was attempting to create a national consensus by steering a political course between the "hard line" military men, who wished to close the Congress and set up a formal dictatorship, and the "soft line" military officials, who felt that the army had performed its function by overturning the Goulart regime and now should return to the barracks. The end of this experiment came after the state elections of October, 1965. The government had permitted elections to be held freely in eleven states, and the results generally indicated a dissatisfaction with the Administration of President Castelo Branco. The governors elected in two key states, Minas Gerais and Guanabara, were old Vargas henchmen. To many, the election results indicated that the revolution was over and it was "politics as usual." The President, pressured by the "hard line" military, went to the Congress requesting greater powers to deal with the challenge created by the victory of anti-revolutionary governors. When Congress refused, the President issued a second Institutional Act on October 27, 1965, which granted him the powers that had been refused by the legislative branch. In addition, the act dissolved all the existing political parties, and in their place an official government party, National Renovation Alliance (Aliança Renovadora Nacional; ARENA), was created. An official opposition party was also ordered organized. The Brazilian Democratic Movement (Movimento Democrático Brasileiro; MDB) came into existence.

The second Institutional Act also took away from the citizens the right to vote directly for the next President of the country. Article 9 stated that Congress would select the new chief executive. An official government candidate, Marshal Artur da Costa e Silva, a native of Rio Grande do Sul, was thus elected the twenty-second President of Brazil on October 3, 1966, by a unanimous vote of 295 congressmen.

There was no opposition candidate. His inauguration date was set for March, 1967.

Articles 14, 15 and 16 of the second Institutional Act have caused considerable friction between the civilian politicians and the military leaders of the revolution. These articles give the President of the Republic the power to take away the political rights of any citizen considered a threat to the revolution. In effect, these sections of the second Institutional Act are used as a club over the heads of recalcitrant and uncooperative congressmen. Charges may range from subversion to gross corruption.

Shortly after the presidential election of October 3, 1966, President Castelo Branco stripped six MDB congressmen of their political rights. The president of the Chamber of Deputies, though a member of the official government party, ARENA, temporarily broke with Castelo Branco over this use of presidential power. In a rare and unexpected demonstration of congressional independence, the leader of the lower house of the legislature declared that the purged congressmen could continue to serve in Congress despite the presidential decree. This challenge to executive authority and the revolution resulted in the issuing of Complementary Act Number 23 of October 20, 1966, by President Castelo Branco. Congress was ordered closed from October 20 to November 22, 1966. Brazilian army units padlocked the Congress.

Institutional Act Number Three, issued February 3, 1966, declared that state governors would be elected indirectly by the state legislatures.

Thus the only direct participation in national political affairs remaining in the hands of the Brazilian people are the elections for the Chamber of Deputies and Senate scheduled for November 15, 1966. Civilian participation in the decisions of government has been whittled away.

Some three years after the 1964 revolution, the situation in Brazil remains unsettled. In the political sector the revolution has not been a success. The military regime has not been popular, and many feel that the opportunity for a broadly based revolution was stolen by the army. Though an air of apathy is apparent in the population as a whole, constant and open criticism of the government persists throughout the nation. Inflation has been slowed down, but the economic problems faced by the lower income groups has not been alleviated to any considerable extent.

President Castelo Branco has maintained tight control over the political affairs of the country. Late in January, 1967, an obedient and spiritless Congress containing 276 ARENA members as opposed to 131 members of the MDB opposition in the Chamber of Deputies and 42 ARENA supporters and 23 MDB members in the Senate approved a new constitution which gives greater powers to the President and further centralizes the administration of the nation. The 1967 Constitution is a conservative document. The same Congress, just before adjournment, approved a new and stringent press law which puts relatively tight controls on the communications media.

In the first months of 1967 the Brazilian military still dominate the political life of the nation. The civilian opposition is fragmented and demoralized. How long the military can maintain their control without coming into deep conflict with the rising demands of the popular and middle-class sectors is an open-ended question. So far Bazil has avoided violence. But unless some dramatic changes are made by President-elect Artur da Costa e Silva, who takes office in March, 1967, the next few years will be unsettled ones. There is a quickening of pace in Brazil as the problems increase and it becomes necessary to find solutions and make adjustments more rapidly than in earlier periods. The Brazilian political structure remains amazingly resilient as civilian politicians and military men adjust to new challenges. Whether this tradition can endure under present conditions remains to be seen. Unquestionably, dangerous and trying periods lie ahead.

Notes

Chapter 1: The Colonial and Imperial Background

1. Getúlio Vargas, *Nova política do Brasil* (Rio de Janeiro: Livraria José Olympio Editôra, 1938), I, 63.
2. Bailey W. Diffie, *Prelude to Empire* (Lincoln: University of Nebraska Press, 1960), p. 81.
3. Bailey W. Diffie, *Latin American Civilization* (Harrisburg: Stackpole Sons, 1945), pp. 642–643.
4. Serafim Leite, S.J., *História da Companhia de Jesús no Brasil* (Lisbon: Livraria Portugalia, 1938), I, 19.
5. Roger Bastide, "Religion and the Church in Brazil," in Thomas Lynn Smith and Alexander Marchant, eds., *Brazil: Portrait of Half a Continent* (New York: Dryden Press, 1951), p. 334.
6. Charles R. Boxer, *The Dutch in Brazil* (London: Oxford University Press, 1957), p. 241.
7. Charles R. Boxer, *The Golden Age of Brazil* (Berkeley: University of California Press, 1962), p. 35.
8. Celso Furtado, *The Economic Growth of Brazil* (Berkeley: University of California Press, 1963), p. 81.
9. Caio Prado Junior, *História econômica do Brasil* (São Paulo: Editôra Brasiliense, 1945), p. 48.
10. Afonso Arinos de Melo-Franco, *Estudos de direito constitucional* (Rio de Janeiro: Edição Revista Forense, 1957), p. 244.
11. Clarence H. Haring, *Empire in Brazil* (Cambridge: Harvard University Press, 1958), p. 54.
12. Alan K. Manchester, "Dom Pedro Segundo, the Democratic Emperor," in Lawrence F. Hill, ed., *Brazil* (Berkeley: University of Californa Press, 1947), p. 43.
13. Prado Junior, p. 161.
14. *Ibid.*, p. 171.
15. Haring, pp. 73–74.
16. George C. A. Boehrer, *Da monarquia à república* (Rio de Janeiro: Ministério da Educação e Cultura, Serviço de Documentação, 1954), pp. 285–286.
17. *Ibid.*, p. 247.
18. Hélio Jaguaribe, *Desenvolvimento econômico e desenvolvimento político* (Rio de Janeiro: Editôra Fundo de Cultura, 1962), p. 165.
19. Raymundo Faoro, *Os donos do poder* (Pôrto Alegre: Editôra Globo, 1958), p. 204.

Chapter 2: The Old Republic: 1889 to 1930

1. Boehrer, pp. 285–286.
2. A. Curtis Wilgus, ed., *South American Dictators* (Washington: George Washington University Press, 1937), p. 465.

3. Thomas Lynn Smith, *Brazil: People and Institutions* (Baton Rouge: Louisiana State University Press, 1946), p. 348.
4. Preston E. James, *Brazil* (New York: Odyssey Press, 1942), p. 206.
5. Pedro Calmon, *História social do Brasil* (São Paulo: Companhia Editôra Nacional, 1934), I, 210–211.
6. Alexandre José Barbosa Lima Sobrinho, *A verdade sôbre a revolução de Outubro* (São Paulo: Editôra Gráfica Unitas, 1933), p. 262.
7. João F. Normano, *Brazil: A Study of Economic Types* (Chapel Hill: University of North Carolina Press, 1935), p. 40.
8. Herman Gerlach James, *The Constitutional System of Brazil* (Washington, D.C., Carnegie Institution, 1923), pp. 38–42.
9. Preston E. James, p. 45.
10. *Ibid.*, p. 45.
11. Percy Alvin Martin, "Federalism in Brazil," *Hispanic American Historical Review*, XVIII, No. 2 (1938), 157.
12. Charles W. Turner, *Ruy Barbosa* (New York: Abingdon-Cokesbury Press, 1945), p. 149.
13. *Ibid.*, p. 149.
14. Lawrence F. Hill, ed., *Brazil* (Berkeley: University of California Press, 1947), p. 84.
15. João Pandiá Calogeras, *A History of Brazil*, trans. and ed. by Percy Alvin Martin Chapel Hill: University of North Carolina Press, 1939), p. 313.
16. Letter from Odilon Duarte Braga to Jordan Young, Rio de Janeiro, December, 1949.
17. José Maria dos Santos, *Política geral do Brasil* (São Paulo: J. M. Magalhães, 1930), p. 449.
18. Virgílio A. de Melo-Franco, *Outubro, 1930* (Rio de Janeiro: Editôra Schmidt, 1931), p. 35.
19. Ernest Hambloch, *Report on the Economic and Financial Conditions in Brazil, 1922, 1924, 1925, 1926* (London: H.M. Stationery Office, 1926), p. 17.
20. John Wilkinson Foster Rowe, "Studies in the Artificial Control of Raw Material Supplies," No. 3: *Brazilian Coffee*, London: *Royal Economic Society Memorandum*, No. 34 (1932), 10.
21. *Ibid.*, p. 23.
22. Virgílio A. de Melo-Franco, p. 40.
23. Brígido Tinoco, *A vida de Nilo Peçanha* (Rio de Janeiro: Livraria José Olympio Editôra, 1962), p. 251.
24. Barbosa Lima Sobrinho, p. 4.
25. Jorge Amado, *Vida de Luiz Carlos Prestes* (Buenos Aires: Editorial Claridad, 1942), pp. 101–103.
26. Juarez Távora, *À guisa de depoimento* (São Paulo: Typographia d' "O Combate," 1927), p. 47.
27. João Alberto Lins de Barros, *Memórias de um revolucionário* (Rio de Janeiro: Editôra Civilização, 1953), p. 20.
28. Sertório de Castro, *A república que a revolução destruía* (Rio de Janeiro: Freitas Bastos, 1932), p. 470.
29. Távora, pp. 240–255.
30. Lourival Coutinho, *O General Góes depõe* (Rio de Janeiro: Livraria Editôra Coelho Branco, 2d ed., 1956), p. 16.
31. João Neves da Fontoura, *Memórias* (Pôrto Alegre: Editôra Globo, 1958), I, 323.
32. Coutinho, p. 26.
33. Jorge Amado, p. 14.
34. Hambloch, p. 7.
35. Coutinho, pp. 42, 43.
36. Rowe, p. 70.

37. Gilberto Amado, *Depois da política* (Rio de Janeiro: Livraria José Olympio Editôra, 1960), pp. 5–7.
38. Agnes S. Waddell, "The Revolution in Brazil," *Foreign Policy Association Information Service*, VI, No. 26 (1931).
39. Castro, p. 514.

Chapter 3: The Politicians and the 1930 Revolution

1. Jurandyr Pires Ferreira, *Abaixo às máscaras* (Lisbon: n.i., 1931), p. 31.
2. *Ibid.*, p. 35.
3. Paul Frischauer, *Presidente Vargas* (São Paulo; Companhia Editôra Nacional, 1944), p. 231.
4. Gilberto Amado, *Depois da política*, pp. 3–16. In a penetrating description of President Washington Luís, Amado helps to explain the actions of the President.
5. Barbosa Lima Sobrinho, p. 51.
6. Neves, *Memórias*, I, 14.
7. Wolfgang Hoffman Harnisch, *O Rio Grande do Sul* (Pôrto Alegre: Livraria do Globo, 1941), p. 250.
8. Alzira Vargas do Amaral Peixoto, *Getúlio Vargas, Meu pai* (Pôrto Alegre: Editôra Globo, 2d ed., 1960), p. 6.
9. *Ibid.*, p. 9.
10. Luiz Vergara, *Fui secretário de Getúlio Vargas* (Pôrto Alegre: Editôra Globo, 1960), p. 23.
11. Frischauer, p. 191.
12. Neves, *Memórias*, I, 291.
13. *Ibid.*, p. 298.
14. Hugo Baldessarini, *Crônica de uma época* (São Paulo: Companhia Editôra Nacional, 1957), p. 11.
15. Neves, *Memórias*, I, 256, 361.
16. Gilberto Amado, *Depois da política*, p. 6.
17. Neves, *Memórias*, I, 384.
18. *Ibid.*, p. 393.
19. Amaral Peixoto, p. 42.
20. João Neves da Fontoura, *Memórias* (Pôrto Alegre: Editôra Globo, 1963), II, 480.
21. Barbosa Lima Sobrinho, p. 61.
22. *Correio Paulistano* (São Paulo), August 9, 1929, p. 2.
23. Barbosa Lima Sobrinho, p. 64.
24. *Ibid.*, p. 66.
25. Aurino Moraes, *Minas na Alliança Liberal e na revolução* (Belo Horizonte: Edições Pindorama, 1933), pp. 24–25.
26. *Jornal do Comércio* (Rio de Janeiro), June 24, 1953, p. 3. Reprints comments made by Flôres da Cunha in Congress on June 23, 1953, concerning these events of 1930.
27. Barbosa Lima Sobrinho, p. 78.
28. Moraes, p. 27.
29. *Correio Paulistano* (São Paulo), August 8, 1929, p. 2.
30. Barbosa Lima Sobrinho, p. 85.
31. Virgílio A. de Melo-Franco, p. 187.
32. André Carrazzoni, *Getúlio Vargas* (Rio de Janeiro: Livraria José Olympio Editôra, 1939), p. 200.
33. Barbosa Lima Sobrinho, p. 122.
34. *Ibid.*, p. 126.
35. Letter from João Neves to Osvaldo Aranha on October 28, 1929, Rio de Janeiro. Copy of the letter in the possession of the author.
36. Barbosa Lima Sobrinho, p. 127.
37. Decoded telegram sent by Osvaldo Aranha to João Neves on December 20, 1929. Copy in possession of the author.

38. *New York Times,* December 27, 1929, p.1. *Correio Paulistano* (São Paulo), December 27, 1929, p. 1.
39. Vargas, pp. 59–63.
40. Ruy Bloem, *A crise da democracia* (São Paulo: Livraria Martins Editôra, 1955), p. 152. The Democratic party of São Paulo had been founded shortly after the 1924 revolution and had been slowly gaining strength in the state.
41. Barbosa Lima Sobrinho, p. 145.
42. Waddell, p. 496.
43. Barbosa Lima Sobrinho, p. 146.
44. Carrazzoni, p. 208.
45. Frischauer, p. 250.
46. Castro, p. 529.
47. Moraes, p. 293. Reprint of interview with Borges de Medeiros in Rio de Janeiro press.
48. *Ibid.*, p. 294.
49. Barbosa Lima Sobrinho, p. 151.
50. No relation to the presidential candidate, Júlio Prestes.
51. Armando Guerra, "The Events in Brazil," *Communist,* IX, No. 11–12 (November–December, 1938), 1031.
52. *Ibid.*, p. 1039.
53. Mauricio de Lacerda, *Segunda república* (Rio de Janeiro: Oficina Gráfica Mundo Médico, Borsoi e Cia, 1931), p. 164.
54. Virgílio A. de Melo-Franco, p. 300.
55. Borges de Medeiros wrote to Getúlio Vargas on June 20, 1930, that, should there be a revolution, "he would be passive but sympathetic," and in no way would the former leader of Rio Grande do Sul combat or restrict any decision that Vargas might take. Copy of letter in the possession of the author.
56. Virgílio A. de Melo-Franco, p. 318.
57. *Diário Nacional* (São Paulo), July 28, 1930, p. 1.
58. Pires Ferreira, p. 94.
59. Barbosa Lima Sobrinho, p. 190.
60. Álvaro de Carvalho, *Nas vésperas da revolução* (São Paulo: Empreza Graphica, 1932), p. 8.
61. Letter of Osvaldo Aranha to Raul Píla, August 28, 1930. Copy in the possession of the author.
62. Santos, p. 475.
63. Vargas, pp. 53–64.
64. Gil de Almeida, *Homens e factos de uma revolução* (Rio de Janeiro: Editôra Calvino Filho, 1932), pp. 304–305.
65. *Diário Nacional* (São Paulo), October 5, 1930.

Chapter 4: The Military and the 1930 Revolution

1. Neves, *Memórias,* II, 97.
2. Gil de Almeida, p. 69.
3. Moraes, p. 293.
4. Copy of cable in author's possession (from Aranha files).
5. Virgílio A. de Melo-Franco, p. 280.
6. *Ibid.*, p. 305.
7. Gil de Almeida, p. 132.
8. Waddell, p. 497.
9. Coutinho, p. 71.
10. Tristão de Alencar Araripe, *Tasso Fragoso, um pouco de história do nosso exército* (Rio de Janeiro: Biblioteca do Exército Editôra, 1960), pp. 544–555.
11. Telegram in possession of the author.
12. Gil de Almeida, p. 212.

13. Anthenor Navarro, "Apontamentos para a história da revolução," *Instituto histórico e geográfico Parahybano*, VII (1932), 29.
14. *New York Times*, August 30, 1930, p. 1.
15. *Ibid.*, September 6, 1930, p. 2.
16. Virgílio A. de Melo-Franco, p. 404.
17. Gil de Almeida, p. 223.
18. *Ibid.*, p. 225.
19. Vargas, pp. 59–63.
20. Virgílio A. de Melo-Franco, p. 433.
21. During this siege Góes Monteiro, writing under the code name of Cívico, began to worry about Vargas' apparent indecision and wrote to Aranha that some definite understanding should be reached with Vargas. Góes wrote, "No one has more responsibility than you for this revolution." Letter in possession of the author from the file of Aranha.
22. United States Department of State, *Papers Relating to the Foreign Relations of the United States* (Washington, D.C.: Government Printing Office, 1945), p. 439.
23. General Estevão Leitão de Carvalho, *Dever militar e política partidária* (São Paulo: Companhia Editôra Nacional, 1959), p. 195. There is a running historical controversy concerning the battle of Itararé. Many observers doubt that any battle took place. General Leitão de Carvalho, writing about the federal army in São Paulo, states categorically, "In the Itararé region, where Paulista territory meets Paraná [federal forces], under the command of a colonel with an excellent professional reputation never went into action." Yet Góes Monteiro refused any suggestion that Itararé was not the scene of a violent struggle. When I interviewed him in Washington on August 23, 1951, he drew diagrams showing troop positions and insisted that a bloody battle took place. There is little hard evidence to prove or disprove what actually happened at Itararé, but the general consensus of informed opinion indicates that nothing similar to contemporary descriptions such as appeared in the press or in United States consular dispatches to Washington actually occurred.
24. United States Department of State, *Papers Relating* . . . , p. 439.
25. Menotti Mucelli, *A revolução em Bello Horizonte* (Belo Horizonte: Typographia Americana, 1930), p. 36.
26. Carvalho, p. 59.
27. *Excelsior* (Mexico City), October 9, 1930, p. 3.
28. United States Department of State, *Press Releases*, Publication No. 124, Weekly Issue No. 56, Saturday, October 25, 1930 (Washington, D.C.: Government Printing Office, 1930), p. 124.
29. United States Department of State, *Papers Relating* . . . , p. 443.
30. Virgílio A. de Melo-Franco, p. 437.
31. Moraes, p. 443.
32. Laurita Pessôa Raja Gabaglia (Irmã Maria Regina do Santo Rosário, o.c.d.), *O Cardeal Leme* (Rio de Janeiro: Livraria José Olympio Editôra, 1962), pp. 216–226.
33. Virgílio A. de Melo-Franco, p. 452.
34. *Ibid.*, p. 443.

Chapter 5: The Collapse of the Coffee Economy

1. Great Britain Department of Overseas Trade, *Report of the British Economic Mission to Argentina, Brazil and Uruguay* (London: H.M. Stationery Office, 1930), p. 28.
2. Rowe, p. 85.
3. *Ibid*, p. 8.
4. Waddell, p. 498.

5. The Bank of Brazil is not a central bank as the term is used in the United States. The Brazilian government held a controlling interest in the bank. The bank acted as agent for the federal government in regard to exchange operations in order to maintain the rate that also regularizes the stabilization of the exchange and extends credit to other banks.
6. Rowe, p. 53.
7. *Tea and Coffee Journal,* LVII (November, 1929), 631. (Italics added.)
8. Barbosa Lima Sobrinho, p. 105.
9. The term "valorization" was introduced into English-speaking countries about 1906 from Brazil, where it had been applied to measures regulating the marketing of coffee. In its original meaning it signified the act or process of raising the price of a commodity, by government interference, above a level regarded as uneconomically low but not above the price that would in the long run be set by free competition. Valorization is presumably temporary in character, and it is significant that when Brazil inaugurated the permanent plan for the control of coffee in 1922, this was described as "defense" of coffee and not valorization.
10. Rowe, p. 56.
11. Telegram December 11, 1929, from João Neves to Osvaldo Aranha. From the files of Aranha. Copy in possession of the author.
12. *Diário Nacional* (São Paulo), December 12, 1929, p. 2.
13. Affonso de Escragnolle Taunay, *História do Café no Brasil* (Rio de Janeiro: Edição do Departamento Nacional do Café, 1942). XIII, 392.
14. *Tea and Coffee Journal,* LVIII (March, 1930), 340.
15. V. D. Wickizer, *The World Coffee Economy* (Palo Alto: Stanford University Press, 1943), p. 147.
16. The *Diário Nacional,* discussing the same transaction, commented editorially on June 1, 1930, that only $40 million would actually come to Brazil, and this amount would be nowhere near enough to purchase the coffee crop.
17. International Institute of Agriculture, *Coffee in 1931 and 1932: Economic and Technical Aspect* (Rome: Printing Office of the Chamber of Deputies, 1934), p. 38.
18. *Tea and Coffee Journal,* LIX (August, 1930), 161.
19. *Moody's Governments and Municipals,* 1930.
20. *Tea and Coffee Journal,* LIX (August, 1930), 182.
21. *Ibid.,* LIX (September, 1930), 340.
22. *Ibid.,* p. 353.
23. Walter Gay McCreery, *The Coffee Industry in Brazil,* United States Department of Commerce, Trade Promotion Series No. 92 (Washington, D.C.: Government Printing Office, 1930), p. 22.
24. *Ibid.,* p. 22.
25. *Diário Nacional* (São Paulo), July 10, 1930, p. 1.
26. *Ibid.,* May 1, 1930.
27. Max Handman, "The Historical Function of Foreign Investments in Latin America," *Michigan Business Papers,* No. 6, January, 1940, p. 34.
28. *New York Times,* June 2, 1930, p. 42.
29. *Diário Nacional* (São Paulo), August 8, 1930.
30. Alan K. Manchester, *British Preeminence in Brazil: Its Rise and Decline* (Chapel Hill: University of North Carolina Press, 1930), p. 340.
31. Rowe, p. 214.
32. Stanley G. Irving, *Report on Economic and Financial Conditions in Brazil,* Great Britain, Department of Overseas Trade (London: H.M. Stationery Office, 1930), p. 34.
33. Robert W. Dunn, *American Foreign Investments* (New York: Viking Press, 1926), p. 68.
34. *La Nación* (Buenos Aires), October 27, 1930, p. 1.
35. *Jornal do Comércio* (Rio de Janeiro), December 10, 1953, p. 3.

Chapter 6: Vargas and the Political Structure: 1930 to 1945

1. Renato Jardim, *A aventura de Outubro e a invasão de São Paulo* (Rio de Janeiro: Editôra Civilização Brasileira, 2d ed., 1932), p. 175.
2. Castilho Cabral, *Tempos de Jânio e outros tempos* (Rio de Janeiro: Editôra Civilização Brasileira, 1962), p. 14.
3. Bertoldo Klinger, *Narrativas aotobiograficas* (Rio de Janeiro: Edições O Cruzeiro, 1951), VI, 327.
4. Renato Jardim, *Um libello a sustentar* (Rio de Janeiro: Editôra Civilização Brasileira, 1933), p. 22.
5. The bibliography on the 1932 Paulista revolt is vast. The episode has never been treated properly in English. Some of the more significant items are the following:

   Coronel Álvaro de Alencastre, *A revolução de 32 e seus ensinamentos militares* (Rio de Janeiro: Papelaria Velho, 1933);
   Eustachio Alves, *Misérias da política* (Rio de Janeiro, Editôra Alba, 1933);
   João Neves da Fontoura, *Accuso!!* (Rio de Janeiro: n.i., 1933);
   Manoel Osório, *A guerra de São Paulo* (São Paulo: Empreza Editôra Americana, 1932);
   Menotti del Picchia, *A revolução Paulista* (São Paulo: Companhia Editôra Nacional, 1932);
   Capitães Heliodoro Tenorio e Odilon Aquino de Oliveira, *São Paulo contra a dictadura* (São Paulo: Edição Ismael Nogueira, 1932);
   Leven Vampre, *São Paulo: Terra conquistada* (São Paulo: Sociedade Impressora Paulista, 1932).

6. Afonso Arinos de Melo-Franco, *Um Estadista da República* (Rio de Janeiro: Livraria José Olympio Editôra, 1955), III, 1407.
7. Karl Loewenstein, *Brazil under Vargas* (New York: Macmillan, 1942), p. 23.
8. Plínio Salgado, *Livro verde da minha campanha* (Rio de Janeiro: Livraria Clássica Brasileira, 1956), p. 210.
9. Coutinho, pp. 306–327.
10. Charles Gauld, *The Last Titan, Percival Farquhar* (Stanford: Institute of Hispanic American and Luso-Brazilian Studies, 1964), pp. 304–325.
11. Lowenstein, p. 206.
12. Coutinho, p. 430.

Chapter 7: The Search for Stability: 1945 to 1966

1. Themistocles Brandão Cavalcanti, *Manual da Constituição* (Rio de Janeiro: Zahar Editôres, 1960), pp. 31–32, 222.
2. *Jornal do Brasil* (Rio de Janeiro), August 5, 1954, p. 1.
3. *Tribuna da Imprensa* (Rio de Janeiro), August 9, 1954, p. 1.
4. Bento Munhoz da Rocha Netto, *Radiografia de Novembro* (Rio de Janeiro: Editôra Civilização Brasileira, 2d ed., 1961), p. 118.
5. *O Jornal do Rio de Janeiro,* August 25, 1954, p. 12.
6. Rocha Netto, p. 81.
7. Cabral, pp. 142–146.
8. Gileno de Carli, *Anatomia da renúncia* (Rio de Janeiro: Edições O Cruzeiro, 1962), pp. 162–163.
9. Cabral, p. 235.
10. *O Estado de São Paulo,* October 25, 1962, p. 8.
11. Abelardo Jurema, *Sexta-Feira, 13: Os últimos dias do govêrno João Goulart* (Rio de Janeiro: Edições O Cruzeiro, 2d ed., 1964), pp. 139–149.
12. Agostinho Fernandes, *Constituição dos Estados Unidos do Brasil* (Rio de Janeiro: Gráfica Editôra Aurora, 20th ed., 1966), pp. 144–149.

Bibliography

The principal sources used in the preparation of this book were documents, chronicles and contemporary histories, and general works. Brazilian documents comprise telegrams, letters, newspaper interviews given by political leaders, dispatches from military headquarters, speeches of Getúlio Vargas when he was campaigning for President and later proclamations during the 1930 revolution. United States documents include State Department press releases and dispatches from consular agencies. Chronicles and contemporary histories were the richest source of information. Many books were written by persons who participated in the 1930 revolution, and most have a definite bias, but by cautious appraisal and by using more than one book written about the same event, some balance is achieved.

The problem of research on such a recent event as the 1930 revolution is complicated, for much pertinent information has been suppressed for reasons of political security. Since many political and financial fortunes have resulted from the revolution, there is more than just average interest in some quarters in concealing some of the facts.

I. Documents

United States Department of State. *Papers Relating to the Foreign Relations of the United States.* Washington, D.C.: Government Printing Office, 1945.

Contains the dispatches from United States consular agencies in Brazil.

United States Department of State. *Press Releases* (Publication No. 124, Weekly Issue No. 56, Saturday, October 25, 1930). Washington, D.C.: Government Printing Office, 1930.
The proclamation of the arms embargo is printed along with an explanation for the action taken by the State Department.

Vargas, Getúlio. *Nova política do Brasil.* Rio de Janeiro: Livraria José Olympio Editôra, 1938, Vol. I.
The material in this volume consists of the collected speeches of Vargas. As they were printed during the dictatorship, they may have been edited carefully, but the campaign promises of the Liberal Alliance are included.

II. Chronicles and Contemporary Histories

Alencar Araripe, General Tristão de. *Tasso Fragoso: Um pouco de história do nosso exército.* Rio de Janeiro: Biblioteca do Exército Editôra, 1960.
Presents an explanation of the role played by General Tasso Fragoso in the events of 1930.

Alencastre, Coronel Álvaro de. *A revolução de 32 e seus ensinamentos militares.* Rio de Janeiro: Papelaria Velho, 1933.
An active participant in the 1932 revolt against Vargas discusses the military aspects of the incident.

Almeida, General Gil de. *Homens e factos de uma revolução.* Rio de Janeiro: Editôra Calvino Filho, 1932
Contains many interesting letters and messages that were transmitted between Almeida's headquarters in Rio Grande do Sul and the national military headquarters concerning revolutionary activity. The author discusses the role of the Church in regard to war. Almeida was particularly incensed with the Archbishop of Pôrto Alegre for cooperating openly with the revolutionaries.

Almeida, Martins de. *Brasil errado.* Rio de Janeiro; Edição da Organização Simões, 2d ed., 1953.
Written in 1932, this book contains an interesting and valuable description of Brazilian politics of the early 1930's from a São Paulo perspective.

Alves, Eustachio. *Misérias da política.* Rio de Janeiro: Editôra Alba, 1933.

A disillusioned participant in the 1930 revolution presents an attack on the political structure of the country. There are good documents that pertain to the 1930 revolution and an interesting analysis of the military in politics.

Amado, Gilberto. *Depois da política.* Rio de Janeiro: Livraria José Olympio Editôra, 1960.

Reveals much about the personality of Washington Luís and why Getúlio Vargas was selected as his Minister of Finance in 1928.

———. *Perfil do Presidente Getúlio Vargas.* Rio de Janeiro: Imprensa Nacional, 1936.

A flattering official portrait of Vargas written before the dictatorship began.

Amaral, Azevedo. *A aventura política do Brasil.* Rio de Janeiro: Livraria José Olympio Editôra, 1935.

An attempt to explain Brazilian problems by emphasizing the economic factors. Some good comments on the 1934 Constitution.

Amaral Peixoto, Alzira Vargas do. *Getúlio Vargas: Meu pai.* Pôrto Alegre: Editôra Globo, 1960.

Getúlio Vargas' daughter has written a fascinating book describing the politicians who surrounded her father. Many politicians were deeply hurt by statements that appeared in this book.

Assis Brasil, Joaquim Francisco de. *Attitude do Partido Democrático Nacional.* Pôrto Alegre: Livraria do Globo, 1929.

Explains why Assis Brasil was willing to support the Liberal Alliance in the 1930 election.

Barbosa Lima Sobrinho, Alexandre José. *A verdade sôbre a revolução de Outubro.* São Paulo: Editôra Gráfica Unitas, 1933.

The author analyzes the background of the revolution and also presents a number of documents. The book appears to be impartial and presents material that shows both sides of the question. Of the many books studied on the period, this volume seems to be one of the most penetrating and honest.

Cabral, Castilho. *Tempos de Jânio e outros tempos.* Rio de Janeiro: Editôra Civilização Brasileira, 1962.

Though the primary focus is Jânio Quadros, the book contains some excellent material on São Paulo politics of the 1950's.

Carli, Gileno de. *Anatomia da renúncia.* Rio de Janeiro: Edições O Cruzeiro, 1962.

Separates fact from fiction regarding the desertion of Jânio Quadros from the presidential office.

Carvalho, Álvaro de. *Nas vésperas da revolução.* São Paulo: Empreza Graphica, 1932.

This book is essential for the events shortly after the death of João Pessôa in Paraíba. The author became governor of the state when João Pessôa was assassinated, and his reaction to the messages from Governor Vargas relating to federal troops in the state are interesting.

Color, Lindolfo. *As opposições Sul-Rio-Grandenses e o movimento militar de São Paulo.* Rio de Janeiro: Pimenta de Mello e Cia., 1925.

The author was a brilliant young politician from the state of Rio Grande do Sul, who died shortly after the revolution. The book treats the 1924 revolution in detail as it affected the state of Rio Grande do Sul.

Coutinho, Lourival. *O General Góes depõe.* Rio de Janeiro: Livraria Editôra Coelho Branco, 2d ed., 1956.

General Góes Monteiro in a series of interviews gave his opinions about events and personalities who moved across the Brazilian political scene over a period of thirty years. Few documents are available, and in some cases there is disagreement about the manner in which the General remembers an event and the recollection of others who also were present. Must be read to understand the period.

Davis, Horace B. "Brazil's Political and Economic Problems." *Foreign Policy Association Reports*, Vol. XI, No. 1, 1935.

The author, a North American, taught at a Brazilian university for a number of years, and his economic information is penetrating and informative. Occasionally he is too broad and sweeping in his conclusions.

Dunn, Robert W. *American Foreign Investments.* New York: Viking Press, 1926.

A detailed study of American investments abroad. There is less on Latin America and Brazil than desired, but the book fills a gap for the period.

Fragoso, General Tasso. "A revolução de 1930." *Revista do Instituto Histórico e Geográfico Brasileiro,* Vol. CCXI, April–June, 1951.

This material, written in 1935, contains some interesting insights into the military mind and the 1930 revolution. Curious statement on how angry Góes Monteiro was when the military junta took over in Rio de Janeiro on October 24, 1930.

Góes Monteiro, General Pedro Aurélio. *A revolução de 30 e a finalidade política do exército.* Rio de Janeiro: Editôra Anderson, 1934.

Preface by José Américo de Almeida and remarks by General Góes Monteiro on the role of the army in Brazilian politics.

Great Britain, Department of Overseas Trade. *Report of the British Economic Mission to Argentina, Brazil and Uruguay.* London: H.M. Stationery Office, 1930.

A very brief account of the mission sent over by the British to salvage their commercial relations with these countries, which were affected by the depression. Written for British consumption, it disparages North American commercial activity in Latin America.

Hambloch, Ernest. *Report on the Economic and Financial Conditions in Brazil, 1922, 1924, 1925, 1926.* A report prepared for the Great Britain Department of Overseas Trade. London: H.M. Stationery Office, 1926.

These are the yearly reports by the economic section of the British Embassy in Brazil. The material is essential for tracing and understanding the financial and economic events through the 1920's.

Handman, Max. "The Historical Function of Foreign Investments in Latin America." *Michigan Business Papers* No. 6, January, 1940.

A discussion of the role of North American investments in Latin America in very humane and understandable terms. The treatment of the problem is in strictly economic terms, also in its relation to the political stability of the countries involved.

International Institute of Agriculture. *Coffee in 1931 and 1932: Economic and Technical Aspect.* Rome: Printing Office of the Chamber of Deputies, 1934.
The text contains a splendid bibliography listing books on coffee published all over the world. The material leans heavily on an article by J. W. F. Rowe for the Royal Economic Society.

Irving, Stanley G. *Report on the Economic and Financial Conditions in Brazil.* Great Britain, Department of Overseas Trade. London: H.M. Stationery Office, 1930.
The yearly report by the commercial office of the British Embassy in Brazil.

Jurema, Abelardo. *Sexta-Feira, 13: Os últimos dias do govêrno João Goulart.* Rio de Janeiro: Edições O Cruzeiro, 2d ed., 1964.
An extremely detailed account of the last days of the Goulart administration by one of the cabinet ministers.

Klinger, Bertoldo. *Nós e a dictadura.* n.i., 1933.
An explanation of why Klinger joined the São Paulo rebellion in 1932.

———. *Narrativas Aotobiograficas.* Rio de Janeiro: Edições O Cruzeiro, 1951, Vol. VI.
Written by an extremely eccentric military official who was chief of police of Rio de Janeiro after the revolution and later broke with Vargas.

Landucci, Italo. *Cenas e episódios da coluna Prestes.* São Paulo: Editôra Brasiliense, 1947.
A diary of events kept by one of the men in the Luís Carlos Prestes column.

Leitão de Carvalho, General Estevão. *Dever militar e política partidária.* São Paulo: Companhia Editôra Nacional, 1959.
His comments on the role of the army in the political life of the country are very informative.

Leitão de Carvalho, Colonel Estevão. *Na revolução de 30.* Rio de Janeiro: Editôra Schmidt, 1933.
An explanation of the attitude of the author's regiment in the 1930 revolution.

Lins de Barros, João Alberto. *Memórias de um revolucionário.* Rio de Janeiro: Editôra Civilização, 1953.
A cautious recollection by one of the leading 1924 rebels.

Lira, José Pereira. *Servindo a Paraíba.* Rio de Janeiro: Imprensa Nacional, 1935.
A pamphlet which deals with the events of 1930 in the state of Paraíba.

Lombardo Toledano, Vicente. "La revolución del Brasil," *Publicaciones de la Confederación de los Estudiantes Socialistas de México.* Mexico City, 1936.
Contains a number of articles written by the Mexican labor leader through the years 1930 to 1936, which show an interesting development in regard to the treatment of the Brazilian Communist leader Luís Carlos Prestes. He is not mentioned by Lombardo Toledano in the first of the articles, which were written in 1930 in Buenos Aires, but articles written in 1936 call Prestes the great revolutionary leader of Brazil.

McCreery, Walter Gay. *The Coffee Industry in Brazil.* United States Department of Commerce, Trade Promotion Series No. 92. Washington, D.C.: Government Printing Office, 1930.
A detailed study of the coffee industry in 1927 and 1928. A great deal of statistical data is presented and analyzed. A clear treatment of a difficult and complicated subject.

Melo-Franco, Afonso Arinos de. *Um estadista da República.* Rio de Janeiro: Livraria José Olympio Editôra, 1955, Vols. I, II, III.
This biography of Afrânio de Melo-Franco contains excellent descriptions of Minas Gerais political life before 1930 and various aspects of foreign affairs under Vargas.

Melo-Franco, Virgílio A. de. *Outubro, 1930.* Rio de Janeiro: Editôra Schmidt, 1931.
The author cooperated closely with the Liberal Alliance leaders favoring revolution. The book is startling in its frankness of

comment about Vargas and was severely criticized at the time of its third printing in 1932. Later Melo-Franco broke with Vargas and the book was suppressed.

Moraes, Aurino. *Minas na Alliança Liberal e na revolução.* Belo Horizonte: Edições Pindorama, 1933.
Presents the role of Minas Gerais in the revolution. Chiefly interesting for the letters and full texts of parliamentary debates in Minas Gerais.

Mucelli, Menotti. *A revolução em Bello Horizonte.* Belo Horizonte: Typographia Americana, 1930.
A collection of articles that were first published in the newspaper *Estado de Minas.* The focus is on the revolutionary events in the capital of Minas Gerais, Belo Horizonte.

Munhoz da Rocha Netto, Bento. *Radiografia de Novembro.* Rio de Janeiro: Editôra Civilização Brasileira, 2d ed., 1961.
An extremely detailed account of the events of November, 1955. The documents presented are important for an understanding of the period.

Navarro, Anthenor. "Apontamentos para a história da revolução," *Instituto histórico e geográfico Parahybano,* Vol. VII, 1932.
Covers the activities of Juarez Távora in northeastern Brazil. Explains some background of the Paraíba political scene and also what elements promised to cooperate with the military phase of the 1930 revolution.

Neves da Fontoura, João. *Accuso!!* Rio de Janeiro: n.i., 1933.
A blistering attack on the Vargas dictatorship by a former ally of Getúlio Vargas.

———. *A jornada liberal.* Pôrto Alegre: Livraria do Globo, 1932, Vols. I, II.
An interesting introduction by Antônio Carlos Ribeiro de Andrada gives credit to João Neves for being the first person to articulate plans for an armed revolt if the presidential campaign failed. Basically a collection of Neves' speeches in the Brazilian Congress.

Neves da Fontoura, João. *Memórias.* Pôrto Alegre: Editôra Globo. Vol. I, 1958. Vol. II, 1963.

João Neves was one of the crucial figures in the 1930 revolution. His intimate relationship with all aspects of Rio Grande do Sul politics and national affairs makes these volumes very useful for a deeper understanding of the Vargas period.

Osório, Manoel. *A guerra de São Paulo.* São Paulo: Empreza Editôra Americana, 1932.

Interesting comments on São Paulo politics in the period 1930 to 1932, when the Paulista revolt broke out.

Picchia, Menotti del. *A revolução Paulista.* São Paulo: Edições da Companhia Editôra Nacional, 1932.

A beautifully written study of the Paulista revolution which contains more emotion than hard factual material.

Pires Ferreira, Jurandyr. *Abaixo às máscaras.* Lisbon: n.i., 1931.

The volume was published in Lisbon while the author was in exile for opposing the Vargas regime. There is naturally a great deal of anti-Vargas sentiment throughout the book. A number of documents are presented that illustrate the struggle for power between the Church and Masonic elements in the state of Minas Gerais.

Rowe, John Wilkinson Foster. "Studies in the Artificial Control of Raw Material Supplies," No. 3: Brazilian Coffee. London: Royal Economic Society Memorandum, No. 34, 1932.

A detailed study of the coffee problem, with a number of tables and statistical charts. This material cannot be obtained elsewhere, and studies made by Brazilians do not approach this work in objectivity and soundness of reasoning. Most other studies use this report as a base.

Silva, Hélio. *1930–A Revolução Traída.* Rio de Janeiro: Editôra Civilização Brasileira, 1966.

An interesting and comprehensive study of the 1930 revolution which utilizes documents and also incorporates the published memoirs of many of the participants in the events of 1930.

Souza Soares, José de. *Militarismo na República.* Editôra Monteiro Lobato, 1925.

Frankly critical of the role of the military in events shortly after the founding of the Republic. Also covers the 1922 and 1924 military uprisings.

Távora, Juarez. *À guisa de depoimento.* São Paulo: Typographia d' "O Combate," 1927.

An extremely valuable commentary on the 1924 revolution by an important participant.

Tea and Coffee Journal, Vols. LVII–LIX, 1929, 1930.

One of the few trade journals in the United States that carefully followed the daily commercial activity of the coffee industry in the United States and Brazil.

Tenorio, Capitães Heliodoro e Odilon Aquino de Oliveira. *São Paulo contra a dictadura.* São Paulo: Edição Ismael Nogueira, 1932.

Detailed information of the planning for the 1932 Paulista revolution.

Tinoco, Brígido. *A vida de Nilo Peçanha.* Rio de Janeiro: Livraria José Olympio Editôra, 1962.

An excellent biography of Nilo Peçanha by Luís Jardim, who writes under the pen name of Brígido Tinoco. The 1922 presidential campaign is discussed in the last twenty pages of the book.

Vampre, Leven. *São Paulo: Terra conquistada.* São Paulo: Sociedade Impressora Paulista, 1932.

Good treatment of the João Alberto period in São Paulo.

Vergara, Luiz. *Fui secretário de Getúlio Vargas.* Pôrto Alegre: Editôra Globo, 2d ed., 1960.

Some new information about the events of 1937 and interesting insights into the personality of Getúlio Vargas.

Waddell, Agnes S. "The Revolution in Brazil," *Foreign Policy Association Information Service,* Vol. VI, No. 26, 1931.

The report is well documented from Brazilian newspaper sources and government publications. The author was in Brazil at the time of the revolution and demonstrates a thorough knowledge of Brazilian political life. The newspaper *Estado de São Paulo* and congressional debates are frequently cited.

Wickizer, V. D. *The World Coffee Economy.* Palo Alto: Stanford University Press, 1943.
A well-written report, fully documented with graphs and tables.

III. General Works

Amado, Jorge. *Vida de Luiz Carlos Prestes.* Buenos Aires: Editorial Claridad, 1942.
Gives a good general picture of the Communist leader, Luís Carlos Prestes; however, the book is essentially of the hero-worship type.

Azevedo, Fernando. *Brazilian Culture.* New York: Macmillan, 1950.
Basic for understanding the Brazilian cultural *milieu.*

Baldessarini, Hugo. *Crônica de uma época.* São Paulo: Companhia Editôra Nacional, 1957.
Extremely critical of Getúlio Vargas to the point of sensationalism.

Bello, José Maria. *História da República.* São Paulo: Companhia Editôra Nacional, 4th ed., 1959.
Supplies an excellent background survey of events leading to the revolution. The author's interpretation of political events in the administration preceding Washington Luís, has been particularly helpful.

Bloem, Ruy. *A crise da democracia.* São Paulo: Livraria Martins Editôra, 1955.
A detailed description of political life in São Paulo, pointing out the failure of the political parties.

Boehrer, George C. A. *Da monarquia à república.* Rio de Janeiro: Ministério da Educação e Cultura, Serviço de Documentação, 1954.
Exceptionally perceptive analysis of the role of the Republican party in the transition from the monarchy to the Republic.

Boxer, Charles R. *The Dutch in Brazil.* London: Oxford University Press, 1957.

Extremely well written and thoughtful study of an important period in Brazilian history.

——. *The Golden Age of Brazil.* Berkeley: University of California Press, 1962.

A sharp focus on the years that followed the gold rush in Brazil.

Calmon, Pedro. *História social do Brasil.* 2 vols. São Paulo: Companhia Editôra Nacional, 1934.

The books of Pedro Calmon present an attractive sweep of Brazilian social history.

Calogeras, João Pandiá. *A History of Brazil,* translated and edited by Percy Alvin Martin. Chapel Hill: University of North Carolina Press, 1939.

A good general survey of Brazilian history. The material that covers the modern republican period is generally subject to question, for the author participated actively in the governments and administrations he describes.

Carrazzoni, André. *Getúlio Vargas.* Rio de Janeiro: Livraria José Olympio Editôra, 1939.

The author is an excellent Brazilian journalist, and although his life of Vargas appears to be slanted to put Vargas in a favorable light, many interesting and informative pieces of information are presented.

Castro, Sertorio de. *A república que a revolução destruía.* Rio de Janeiro: Freitas Bastos, 1932.

Contains a detailed account of the early republican history of Brazil. The author is a well-known Brazilian publicist who opposed Vargas and considered him a dictator as early as 1930.

Cavalcanti, Themistocles Brandão. *Manual da Constituição.* Rio de Janeiro: Zahar Editôres, 1960.

A good commentary on the 1946 Constitution.

Diffie, Bailey W. *Latin American Civilization.* Harrisburg: Stackpole Sons, 1945.

One of the best interpretations of the Latin American colonial period.

——. *Prelude to Empire.* Lincoln: University of Nebraska Press, 1960.

Sets the scene for Portuguese overseas expansion.

Faoro, Raymundo. *Os donos do poder.* Pôrto Alegre: Editôra Globo, 1958.

Reaches way back into Portuguese history to show why Brazilian development is so slow and painful. Some interesting observations on Brazilian economics in the colonial period.

Fernandes, Agostinho. *Constituição dos Estados Unidos do Brasil.* Rio de Janeiro: Gráfica Editôra Aurora, 20th ed., 1966.

A very useful and annotated review of the Brazilian constitution. The three Institutional Acts are also available in this last edition.

Freyre, Gilberto. *The Masters and the Slaves.* New York: Alfred A. Knopf, 1946.

The best account of the impact of slavery on Brazilian society.

Frischauer, Paul. *Presidente Vargas.* São Paulo: Companhia Editôra Nacional, 1944.

This book frankly lauds Vargas. Valuable solely for comparison purposes and to see the manner in which the government represented the revolution to the people. The book was distributed free by the government propaganda agency and was considered an official biography of Getúlio Vargas.

Furtado, Celso. *The Economic Growth of Brazil.* Berkeley: University of California Press, 1963.

An interesting economic study of Brazil from the colonial period to the present.

Gauld, Charles. *The Last Titan, Percival Farquhar.* Stanford: Institute of Hispanic American and Luso-Brazilian Studies, 1964.

Contains significant information for researchers on United States business activity in Brazil during the Vargas period.

Guerra, Armando. "The Events in Brazil," *Communist*, Vol. IX, November–December, 1938.

A long article discussing political events in Brazil. Includes a number of letters written by Luís Carlos Prestes to Communist party officials in Russia concerning the 1930 revolution, and some information concerning the size and character of the Communist party as a political factor in Brazil in the 1920's.

Haring, Clarence H. *Empire in Brazil.* Cambridge: Harvard University Press, 1958.

A solid description of the reign of Dom Pedro II.

Harnisch, Wolfgang Hoffman. *O Rio Grande do Sul.* Pôrto Alegre: Livraria do Globo, 1941.

A light survey of Rio Grande do Sul history. Some interesting economic aspects of the state are presented.

Hill, Lawrence F., ed. *Brazil.* Berkeley: University of California Press, 1947.

The treatment of Brazilian history is broken down into chapters in which different phases of Brazilian history, both political and cultural, are described by authorities.

Jaguaribe, Hélio. *Desenvolvimento econômico e desenvolvimento político.* Rio de Janeiro: Editôra Fundo de Cultura, 1962.

By one of the leading younger economic planners of Brazil. He is relatively pessimistic about Brazil's future unless some radical changes are made.

James, Herman Gerlach. *The Constitutional System of Brazil.* Washington: Carnegie Institution, 1923.

A study of the Brazilian Constitution of 1891. The first chapter contains a short survey of Brazilian history, which helps explain many sections of the Constitution. The Brazilian political system is also analyzed.

James, Preston E. *Brazil.* New York: Odyssey Press, 1942.

Extremely valuable. The statistical data are well presented.

Jardim, Renato. *A aventura de Outubro e a invasão de São Paulo.* Rio de Janeiro: Editôra Civilização Brasileira, 2d ed., 1932.

One of the better books on the development of republican

Brazil. Discusses the background to the political and social problems that face the country. The interpretations are penetrating.

Jardim, Renato. *Um libello a sustentar.* Rio de Janeiro: Editôra Civilização Brasileira, 1933.
Partially an answer to the many attacks that were leveled against the author for his earlier book. It also contains an interesting discussion of the role of Cardinal Leme in the 1930 revolution.

Lacerda, Mauricio de. *Segunda república.* Rio de Janeiro: Oficina Gráfica Mundo Médico, Borsoi e Cia., 1931.
The author was an early revolutionary who broke with Vargas when he realized that the rebellion would bring no social or economic changes. He was a representative from the state of Rio de Janeiro to the federal Congress. The chapters that describe the early attempts to reach an agreement with Communist leader Luís Carlos Prestes are effective and informative.

Leite, Serafim. *História da Companhia de Jesús no Brasil.* Lisbon: Livraria Portugalia, 1938, Vol. I.
An exceptionally fine detailed and documented study of the Jesuits in Brazil.

Loewenstein, Karl. *Brazil under Vargas.* New York: Macmillan, 1942.
A good early attempt to describe the political structure of Brazil during the Vargas dictatorship. Gives some indication of the difference between Brazilian theory and practice.

Manchester, Alan K. *British Preeminence in Brazil: Its Rise and Decline.* Chapel Hill: University of North Carolina Press, 1930.
The book is good for the colonial and monarchy periods. The role of investment capital in the coffee industry, which was the backbone of the Brazilian financial structure from the 1880's to 1930, is not discussed.

Martin, Percy Alvin. "Federalism in Brazil," *Hispanic American Historical Review*, Vol. XVIII, No. 2, 1938.
Discusses the development of the federalist ideas in Brazil. The changes that have taken place in Brazilian political life are presented with significant interpretations.

Medeiros, Mauricio de. *Outras revoluções virão.* Rio de Janeiro: Oficina Gráfica Mundo Médico, Borsoi e Cia., 1932.

An interesting analysis of the presidential government in pre-1930 Brazil. It claims that one of the most important reasons for the revolution was the opposition to a strong chief executive.

Melo-Franco, Afonso Arinos de. *Estudos de direito constitucional.* Rio de Janeiro: Edição Revista Forense, 1957.

Contains eight studies written between 1949 and 1956 on such subjects as political parties, the presidential versus the parliamentary systems of government and freedom of the press in Brazil.

Normano, João F. *Brazil: A Study of Economic Types.* Chapel Hill: University of North Carolina Press, 1935.

The author has made important compilations of Brazilian economic data. From this material many generalizations on Brazilian economic life have been made. Some of the material that Normano gathered together in tables appears in the later works of such Brazilian economists as Caio Prado Junior, and Roberto Simonsen.

Prado Junior, Caio. *História econômica do Brasil.* São Paulo: Editôra Brasiliense, 1945.

The author is an economic historian whose books are ultranationalistic. The development of the coffee industry is well presented, but there are no footnotes and a number of statistical tables which first appeared in Normano's book are utilized.

Raja Gabaglia, Laurita Pessôa (Irmã Maria Regina do Santo Rosário, o.c.d.). *O Cardeal Leme.* Rio de Janeiro: Livraria José Olympio Editôra, 1962.

Presents interesting and new material on the political activities of the Church during the Vargas regime. The chapter dealing with the 1930 revolution describes the Cardinal's role in Washington Luís' capitulation to the military.

Salgado, Plínio. *O Integralismo perante a nação.* Rio de Janeiro: Livraria Clássica Brasileira, 3rd ed., 1955.

Some early documents on the founding of the Integralist party. Also includes the opinion of Tristão de Ataíde concerning Integralism.

Salgado, Plínio. *Livro verde da minha campanha.* Rio de Janeiro: Livraria Clássica Brasileira, 1956.

Interesting comments on the political situation in Brazil in 1955 from the Integralista point of view. The eleven documents at the end of the book are valuable.

Santos, José Maria dos. *Política geral do Brasil.* São Paulo: J. M. Magalhães, 1930.

Most of the book is concerned with an analysis of the background of the republic and the character of Brazilian political life. The author believes that one of the prime reasons for the success of the Vargas movement was the decision of the Washington Luís government to draft civilians to fight the revolution.

Schmalhausen, Samuel D., ed. *Recovery through Revolution.* New York: Covici-Friede Publishers, 1933.

Arnold Rollers' chapter, "Whirlwinds of Rebellion in South America," is a leftwing newspaperman's analysis of the Vargas revolution.

Smith, Thomas Lynn. *Brazil: People and Institutions.* Baton Rouge: Louisiana State University Press, 1946.

The author, a rural sociologist, traveled over a considerable part of Brazil and amassed for the first time a great deal of raw information that had never been presented to English-speaking audiences. The information concerning Brazilian rural conditions is a great addition to an understanding of Brazilian social conditions.

Smith, Thomas Lynn, and Alexander Marchant, eds. *Brazil: Portrait of Half a Continent.* New York: Dryden Press, 1951.

Many Brazilian specialists contributed chapters to this valuable study of Brazil.

Taunay, Affonso de Escragnolle. *História do café no Brasil.* Rio de Janeiro: Edição do Departamento Nacional do Café, 1942, Vol. XIII.

An exhaustive history of coffee cultivation in Brazil.

Turner, Charles W. *Ruy Barbosa.* New York: Abingdon-Cokesbury Press, 1945.

A good introductory account of the life of one of Brazil's most important statesmen.

Wilgus, A. Curtis, ed. *South American Dictators*. Washington, D.C.: George Washington University Press, 1937.
An attempt to analyze the dictator problem in Latin America in the mid-1930's. Special attention is paid to Brazil, with the book stating that Vargas was different from other dictators.

IV. Newspapers

The following newspapers were consulted for material pertinent to the October, 1930, revolution.

Correio do Povo, Pôrto Alegre. January, 1929–December, 1930.
An opposition newspaper to the Vargas group.

Correio Paulistano, São Paulo. January, 1929–November, 1930.
The official organ of the Republican party of São Paulo and the coffee planters of the state.

Diário Nacional, São Paulo. January, 1929–December, 1930.
Opposition newspaper against the government of Júlio Prestes and Washington Luís. It favored the tiny Democratic party of São Paulo.

O Estado de São Paulo. January, 1929–November, 1930.
An independent newspaper that was often highly critical of the actions of Júlio Prestes and the Republican party of São Paulo.

A Federação, Pôrto Alegre. May, 1929–December, 1930.
Represented the official Republican party position in Rio Grande do Sul.

Jornal do Rio de Janeiro. May, 1929–December, 1930.
Frankly and openly favored the Liberal Alliance.

La Nación, Buenos Aires. October 1–4, 1930.
The Argentine press covered the Brazilian revolution in considerable detail.

The New York Times. December, 1929–November, 1930.
The paper has been a good barometer of political conditions in Brazil. In the late 1920's and early 1930's the *Times* carried

little material on Brazil when conditions were stable, but usually gave front page attention to any revolution.

A Noite, Rio de Janeiro. May, 1929–December, 1930.
Independent newspaper that tended to be pro-Liberal Alliance.

The following newspapers were consulted for contemporary events during the years 1954 to 1966.

O Estado do São Paulo.
Continues to express a São Paulo point of view on domestic problems. Early enthusiasm for the 1964 revolution has cooled during the past years.

Jornal do Brasil, Rio de Janeiro.
An extremely independent newspaper that continued to criticize the military after 1964.

Jornal do Comércio, Rio de Janeiro.
A conservative newspaper that published historical articles by important political figures.

O Jornal do Rio de Janeiro.
A leading paper of the Diários Associados, one of the most powerful newspaper chains in Brazil.

Tribuna da Imprensa, Rio de Janeiro.
At one time the newspaper of Carlos Lacerda.

Index

About the Author

JORDAN M. YOUNG did his undergraduate work at the University of Illinois, the University of São Paulo, and the University of California, Berkeley, and was subsequently awarded two fellowships for study in Chile and Brazil. Before his Army service in World War II he worked as a rural sociologist in the interior of Brazil for the Special Public Health Service of the Coordinator of Inter-American Affairs. After receiving his Ph.D. degree from Princeton University in 1953 he joined the Chase Bank affiliate in Rio de Janeiro and worked in the Brazilian stock market for nearly two years. During the year 1955–56 he was manager of a small chemical firm in Caracas. Since that time he has taught Latin American history at Pace College, New York City, with time out for several trips to Brazil and visiting professorships at New York University and the City College of New York.